Harford Montgomery Hyde was born in Belfast in 1907 and is the author of more than forty books, mostly biographies and studies in criminology and sociology. He was educated at Sedbergh, Queen's University, Belfast and Magdalen College, Oxford and — besides his secret intelligence work — has practised as a barrister, was Ulster Unionist MP for North Belfast 1950-59, and was Professor of History at the University of the Punjab in Lahore. He is married and lives with his wife at Tenterden, Kent.

Also available from Futura
A TANGLED WEB

H. MONTGOMERY HYDE

GEORGE BLAKE
SUPERSPY

Futura

A Futura Book

For Kenneth

This edition published in 1988 by
Futura Publications, a Division of
Macdonald & Co (Publishers) Ltd
London & Sydney

ISBN 0 7088 3992 4

Printed and bound in Great Britain by
The Guernsey Press Co. Ltd, Guernsey, Channel Islands

Futura Publications
A Division of
Macdonald & Co (Publishers) Ltd
Greater London House
Hampstead Road
London NW1 7QX

A member of Maxwell Pergamon Publishing Corporation plc

Contents

Illustrations

Introduction

DUTCH born George Blake's conviction at his trial which took place mostly in camera at the Old Bailey in 1961, when he pleaded guilty to spying for the Russians between 1951 and 1959, incurred a sentence of forty-two years' imprisonment, a term unprecedented in modern times. Nothing had been publicly known about Blake hitherto except that as a Vice-Consul in the British Foreign Service in Seoul he had been interned for three years with the Minister and other members of the Legation staff by the Communists in North Korea during the Korean War.

In 1966 Blake's sensational escape from Wormwood Scrubs prison, a feat in which the Russians contrary to the general impression were not concerned, prompted a former Austrian intelligence agent, who wrote under the name of E. H. Cookridge, to investigate Blake's career. This he did in four books, to a considerable extent repetitious, published between 1962 and 1970, and based on public sources and conversations with Blake's acquaintances and fellow prison inmates. Cookridge's writings were supplemented by Seán Bourke, the Irish ex-prisoner who organized Blake's escape, of which he wrote a detailed account, also describing the time he later spent with Blake in Moscow before he returned to Dublin where he successfully contested a British application for his extradition. Seán Bourke's book *The Springing of George Blake* appeared in the same year (1970) as the last of Cookridge's four works *George Blake Double Agent*.

In view of the substantial amount of relevant unpublished material which has since become available, besides material not readily accessible, such as interviews which Blake gave to reporters on the Soviet government newspaper *Izvestia* in Russian, it seemed to me that a fresh study of Blake (whom I had once met briefly in Berlin), and his activities in the field of espionage, was due. Hence my own book.

I am particularly grateful to Mr Kenneth de Courcy (Duc de Grantmesnil) for his generosity in putting at my disposal copies of the unpublished documents concerning Blake and his associations from the collection which he has deposited in the Hoover Institution of War, Revolution and Peace at Stanford University, California. These include a long memorandum which Mr de Courcy wrote in Wormwood Scrubs and was able to smuggle out of the prison on his release. I am likewise indebted to Mr Kevin O'Connor of Radio Telefís Eireann for his information on Seán Bourke and Blake as well as the use of his radio feature *A Death in January* broadcast after Bourke's death in 1982.

The Revd Robin Denniston of the Oxford University Press has kindly let me see and quote from the interesting report he wrote on Blake's unpublished autobiography *No Abiding City*, after he had read the script in the Ministry of Foreign Trade in Moscow.

For Blake's experiences in Korea I have derived considerable assistance from *Captive in Korea* by Philip Deane, the *Observer* foreign correspondent.

My thanks are also due to John Farquharson Ltd for permission to quote from *The Springing of George Blake* by Seán Bourke (Cassell, 1970), and also for permission to reproduce photographs between pages 160 and 161 from the same source.

In addition I wish to thank the following who have helped me in various ways: Rupert Allason (Nigel West), Andrew Best, Margaret Duff, Nicholas Elliott, Lord Hutchinson QC, Sophie Lannes, Donald McCormick (Richard Deacon), H. Chapman Pincher, and Nicolas Walter. Finally to my wife, as with so many of my previous books, my gratitude is boundless for her invaluable work in typing and retyping the text.

I ought to add that I have not improvised any of the conversations which have been recorded in the following pages. Their sources have all been authenticated.

H.M.H.
May 1987

The Betrayal

I

SHORTLY after ten o'clock on the morning of 3 May 1961, the Lord Chief Justice of England, Lord Parker, entered Court No 1 at London's Central Criminal Court in the Old Bailey and took his seat on the Bench. The Attorney-General, Sir Reginald Manningham-Buller QC, MP, was already sitting in his seat, as was the leading defence counsel, Mr Jeremy Hutchinson QC. Sir Theobald Mathew, the Director of Public Prosecutions, occupied a place in front of counsel's seats, his presence being due to the importance of the case to be tried. Also present were two gentlemen in the well of the courtroom whom few if any of the spectators or the press recognized as the heads of the two secret services – Sir Dick White of MI6 (Intelligence) and Sir Roger Hollis of MI5 (Security and Counter-Espionage).

The press gallery was full, but there were not many people in the public gallery, since the British press and other media had been served with so-called D notices (D for Defence) by Rear-Admiral George Pirie Thomson in his capacity as Secretary of the Services Press and Broadcasting Committee, requesting all editors of newspapers, periodicals and news agencies including television and radio to co-operate in withholding certain information about the defendant, particularly the fact that he had worked for four years as an agent of MI6 in Berlin. As a result the only notice which had appeared in the newspapers was a brief one issued by the Chief Metropolitan Magistrate, Sir Robert Blundell, who committed the accused for trial, to the effect that 'George Blake, thirty-eight, a Government official, of no fixed address' was to be tried on charges under the Official Secrets Act.

A few minutes later, the accused, who answered to the name of George Blake, was ushered into the dock from the cells below. Of medium height and build, he looked younger than his age, and was clean-shaven, having dispensed with the beard which he had worn in the only press photographs available, taken before the trial. He now appeared in a dark grey suit, with a check shirt and a blue tie with red spots. His dimpled face was sun-burned, and his long dark hair was parted low on the left side. He looked impassively at the judge, as the Clerk of the Court read out the indictment.

This charged him with five counts under the Official Secrets Act, in that 'for a purpose prejudicial to the safety of the interests of the State, he communicated to another person information which might have been useful to an enemy', the offences having taken place in November 1951 and on other specific dates between September 1953 and September 1959. When the accused was asked whether he pleaded 'Guilty' or 'Not Guilty', his reply was scarcely audible – 'Guilty, sir.'

The Attorney-General then rose to state the prosecution's case. 'The charges to which the accused has pleaded guilty are of a very serious character,' the Attorney declared in solemn tones. 'I shall tell the court a little about them in open court, and about his history. Until these matters came to light, it was right to say that Blake enjoyed the reputation of a good character. In October 1943, the defendant, who was a British subject, volunteered for service in the Royal Navy, and served until 1948, when he was demobilized. From that date until his arrest, he was employed in the Government service, both in this country and overseas.'

Pointing to a pile of papers in front of him and addressing the judge, the Attorney went on: 'As your Lordship knows from the depositions, he has made a complete and detailed confession. That is Exhibit One and no doubt you have read it. Its contents, except for the short passages to which I propose to refer, must remain secret, and if there is any question of referring to the confession, apart from those parts I shall mention, I shall have to ask you to close the Court and sit *in camera*.' Counsel went on:

In that statement Blake says that more than ten years ago his philosophical and political views underwent a change, and in the autumn of 1951 he held the strong conviction that the Communist system was the better one and deserved to triumph. To quote his own words, he resolved to join the Communists' side in establishing what he believed to be a balanced and more just society.

Having reached this conclusion he did not take the course of resigning from the Government service. What he did was to approach the Russians and volunteer to work for them. His offer was accepted, and I use his own words, he agreed to make available to the Soviet Intelligence Service such information as came his way in the course of his duties in order to promote the cause of Communism. It appears from his statement that for the past nine-and-a-half years, while employed in the Government service and drawing his salary from the State, he had been working for the Russians as a spy for them and communicating a mass of information to them. In short for the past nine-and-a-half years he had been engaged in betraying his country.

I cannot publicly reveal the nature of the information he has communicated, but in his statement he says this, and again I quote his own words: 'I must freely admit that there was not an official document of any importance to which I had access which was not passed to my Soviet contacts.'

'And he had access to information of great importance,' the Attorney-General stressed. However, the Attorney added, 'although he held responsible positions, his employment fortunately did not give him access to any information relating to secret weapons or nuclear or atomic energy, but it is the case that he has done most serious damage to the interests of this country . . . It is not necessary for me to say anything more at this stage on behalf of the prosecution.'

The Lord Chief Justice then asked the Attorney-General if he now wished the Court to be closed, and Sir Reginald replied that he understood that defence counsel would be better able to submit his plea of mitigation if this were done.

'I have a strong dislike of hearing anything *in camera*,' Lord Parker observed, looking at counsel, 'but I gather you are both satisfied that it would be better?'

Asked if this were so, Mr Hutchinson agreed. 'I am told that much of which I wish to say should not be said in public,' said defence counsel. 'Therefore, my choice must be whether the full facts should be put before you, or whether I should leave out much that should be said, but at least some mitigation should be known to the world in general. That is the choice I have had to make this morning, because I had no idea that these proceedings were going to be held in public. In those circumstances my client wishes, in spite of the disadvantages in many ways to him, that I should have complete freedom to address your Lordship on all matters.'

The judge thereupon ordered the Court to be cleared, after which everyone not connected in some way with the trial left the courtroom. Wooden shutters were then placed on the glass-panelled swing doors and on all windows, while police constables took up positions in the corridors outside Court No 1 to prevent anyone from entering.

The Court was reopened to the general public fifty-three minutes later, after Mr Hutchinson had concluded his plea of mitigation. The Clerk of the Court then rose and addressing the defendant said: 'You have been convicted of felony. Is there anything you wish to say why sentence should not be passed on you according to law?' Blake shook his head, mouthing the word 'No', which was practically inaudible.

The Lord Chief Justice then proceeded to pass sentence. 'Your full written confession reveals that for some years you have been working continuously as an agent and spy for a foreign Power,' the judge told the man standing in the dock. 'Moreover, the information communicated, though not of a scientific nature, was clearly of the utmost importance to that Power and has rendered much of this country's efforts completely useless. Indeed, you yourself have said in your confession that there was not an official document of any importance to which you had access which was not passed on to your Soviet contact.'

The judge continued:

When one realizes that you are a British subject, albeit not by birth,[1] and that throughout this period you were employed by this country – your country – in responsible positions of trust, it is clear that your case is akin to treason. Indeed, it is one of the worst that can be envisaged other than in time of war. It would clearly be contrary to the public interest for me to refer in sentencing you to the full contents of your confession. I can, however, say, without hesitation, that no one who has read it could possibly fail to take that view.

I have listened to all that has been so ably said on your behalf and I fully recognize that it is unfortunate for you that many matters urged in mitigation cannot be divulged. But I can say this, that I am perfectly prepared to accept that it was not for money that you did this, but because of your conversion to a genuine belief in the Communist system. Everyone is entitled to their own views, but the gravamen of the case against you is that you never resigned, that you retained your employment in positions of trust in order to betray your country.

You are not yet thirty-nine years of age. You must know and appreciate the gravity of the offences to which you have pleaded guilty. Your conduct in many countries would undoubtedly carry the death penalty. In our law, however, I have no option but to sentence you to imprisonment, and for your traitorous conduct extending over so many years there must be a very heavy sentence.

The judge went on to point out that for a single offence of the kind the defendant had committed the highest penalty laid down was fourteen years' imprisonment, and he could not, therefore, even if so minded, send him to prison for life. However, the judge continued,

[1] Strictly speaking incorrect. Blake was born in Holland but his father was a naturalized Briton at the time of his birth, which would have made him a British subject by birth, although his mother was Dutch.

[15]

Blake had pleaded guilty to five counts, each dealing with separate periods in his life during which he was betraying his country.

'The Court will impose upon you a sentence of fourteen years' imprisonment on each of the five counts: one, two and three will be consecutive, and those in respect of counts four and five will be concurrent, making a total of forty-two years' imprisonment.' In other words, the defendant would remain in prison until the year 2000, when he would be over eighty.

There was a gasp of astonishment from some of those in court, particularly the representatives of the press and the media, since there was no precedent for such a sentence, which was the longest passed in modern British criminal history.

2

What precisely had George Blake done to deserve such phenomenal punishment? The newspapers and the public generally could only speculate. Questions were immediately put down by backbenchers of all sides in the House of Commons to the Prime Minister, then Mr Harold Macmillan, later Lord Stockton. However, the Prime Minister decided to anticipate his questioners by making a statement which he did after Question Time on 5 May. At the outset he was interrupted by the Independent Labour MP, Emrys Hughes, to the effect that the Blake case was still *sub judice* and that anything the Prime Minister said might prejudice any appeal Blake might make. But he was over-ruled by the Speaker and the Prime Minister was allowed to continue. Responding to Labour pressure, Mr Macmillan refused to divulge the facts of the case on the grounds of national security. At the same time he declared that he was prepared to reveal them to the Leader of the Opposition, Mr Hugh Gaitskell, and any Privy Counsellors he might wish to have associated with him. It was understood that they would not pass on any of the information, but that they would be in a position to assure the Labour Party as a whole that the Government was not withholding anything for party-political purposes but only for genuine security reasons. Mr Gaitskell accepted the Prime Minister's offer and nominated five of his colleagues in the Shadow Cabinet who were members of the Privy Council. They were Gaitskell's deputy, George Brown, two former Defence Ministers, Emmanuel Shinwell and Lord Alexander of Hillsborough, and two former Foreign Secretaries, Herbert (Lord) Morrison and Patrick Gordon Walker. However, when he saw Gaitskell, which he did on the evening of 4 May, the Prime Minister persuaded him to drop Morrison and Gordon Walker, and the meeting took place without them, although Mr Macmillan insisted that it should be attended by the Secretary of the Cabinet, Sir Norman Brook.

Meanwhile, two days after the trial, Blake's solicitor Mr A. E. Cox told a newspaper reporter that his client was devastated by the severity of his sentence, since he had been advised to plead guilty on the ground that he would 'get off more lightly'. He had collapsed in his cell and had been admitted to the prison hospital at Wormwood Scrubs, where the solicitor visited him. The upshot of this meeting was that Blake decided to lodge an appeal against the sentence.

The appeal was heard by the Court of Criminal Appeal on 19 June 1961. Sitting with Mr Justice Hilbery, the senior Queen's Bench judge, were Mr Justice Ashworth and Mr Justice Paul. The prisoner was not well enough to be brought from Wormwood Scrubs for the hearing, which for three-quarters of an hour was heard *in camera*. At the beginning of the open session Mr Justice Hilbery declared that the only ground for the appeal was that the sentence was too severe, and he added that the Court had read all the submissions made by the defence at the Old Bailey.

'The effect of that sentence is to cover the rest of the applicant's natural life,' said Mr Jeremy Hutchinson QC, who again appeared for Blake. 'The sentence raises a matter of fundamental importance, not only to the applicant but to the administration of British justice. In my submission the sentence is inordinate, unprecedented and manifestly excessive. To pass consecutive sentences of fourteen years is wrong in principle.'

Blake's counsel went on to complain that substantial mitigating circumstances concerning Blake's conduct had been given no weight by the Lord Chief Justice in passing sentence, and he asked to be allowed to refer to some of the relevant factors in open session in the light of speculation particularly by the press. But Mr Justice Hilbery refused on behalf of the Appeal Court. 'We are not concerned with press conjecture,' said the judge. 'We are not here to scotch some rumour. We are here to consider whether this sentence was wrong in principle or manifestly excessive. What difference does it make to the applicant whether certain submissions were made in public or private?'

It was in vain for defence counsel to refer to the Prime Minister's statement that Blake had not done irreparable damage and that he had not had access to secret information on nuclear or atomic matters, unlike the atom bomb spy Fuchs who was only sentenced to fourteen years; Blake's sentence was tantamount literally to imprisonment for life, differing from the normal term of life imprisonment for murder which often amounted to a mere ten years as a result of review by the Home Secretary and remission for good conduct. It was the same when Mr Hutchinson described Blake's war work and his subsequent harsh experiences in a prison camp in Korea where his reading matter was restricted to the works of Marx, Engels, Lenin and Stalin.

'He has not been condemned for having a particular political ideology,' Mr Justice Hilbery remarked. 'He has been condemned for remaining in the service of this country, and, in a way which is particularly odious, surreptitiously attempting to do this country as much harm as it was in his power.'

'But that is the essence of his creed,' defence counsel replied. 'This form of philosophy is a form of religion. Blake instructed me that, when the distasteful moment came for him to make his choice, it was his duty to stay where he was and do what he did.'

'This sentence is so inhuman,' Jeremy Hutchinson concluded in his final plea, 'that it is alien to all the principles on which a civilized country would treat its subjects.'

The Court was unmoved by defence counsel's arguments, dismissing the appeal, and agreeing with the Lord Chief Justice that Blake's case was one of the worst that could be envisaged in times of peace. Upholding Lord Parker's forty-two years' sentence, the Court subsequently stated that the sentence had a threefold purpose – punitive, deterrent and intended to safeguard this country.

On the same day as the appeal was heard, Mr Chapman Pincher, defence correspondent of the *Daily Express*, entertained the Rt Hon George Brown PC, MP, to lunch in a well-known London restaurant. No sooner were they seated than Brown told his host the whole story, adding, somewhat to Pincher's surprise, that he could use it in his paper, provided the source was unattributable. First, Blake had given the Russians the names of over forty secret agents working for Britain abroad, mostly behind the Iron Curtain, where as a result many had been captured and shot. That was the main reason for the severity of the sentence, which worked out at approximately a year for each agent the spy had betrayed.

Secondly, while working in West Berlin, Blake had given the KGB photographs of every secret document which passed through his office. Some of this information had enabled the KGB to kidnap prominent East Germans who had defected to the West and take them back behind the Berlin Wall. Thirdly, he had revealed details of a 350-foot-long tunnel which the Americans had bored under the Soviet sector of Berlin to plug into Soviet telephone cables. Finally, Blake had tried to warn the KGB that the professional Soviet spy Gordon Lonsdale and other agents, in what came to be known as the Navy secrets spy ring at Portland, were about to be arrested by the British authorities. It was the interception of this message which led to Blake's recall from his overseas posting to London and his own arrest.

To be on the safe side Chapman Pincher consulted Admiral Thomson who somewhat surprisingly assured him that there was no objection to this information being published. So next day, 20 June 1961, Pincher's scoop appeared on the front page of the *Daily Express* and caused a nation-wide sensation.

3

According to his birth certificate, George Behar, who subsequently changed his surname to Blake, was born at 3.0 pm on 11 November 1922 at his parents' home, 104 Gedempte Botersloot, in Rotterdam.

His father, Albert William Behar, a naturalized British subject and a native of Cairo, was a thirty-three-year-old trader in sports goods, who belonged to the Jewish sect of Sephardim, who were regarded as aristocrats among the Jews and in England included families with such names as Sassoon, Henriques, Montefiore, Swaythling, Samuel and Bearsted. Albert's father was a banker and financial adviser to the Khedive of Egypt. Albert Behar obtained British nationality because Egypt was then under British protection. In the First World War he served as a captain with conspicuous gallantry when he was wounded twice and badly gassed, receiving British and French decorations, the OBE and the Legion of Honour. He later served on Field-Marshal Haig's Intelligence Staff.

In 1919, through a titled friend in London, Albert Behar met a young Dutch girl Catherine Beijderwellen, with whom he fell in love. Catherine came from an equally distinguished but different background in her own country, her family supplying public servants, naval commanders, and Church dignitaries for several centuries. The couple had some difficulty with their respective families who at first did not approve of their proposed match but eventually relented. Thus Albert Behar and Catherine Beijderwellen were married in London on 11 January 1922. Their first child, born exactly ten months later, was named George, in honour of King George V.

The young couple settled in Rotterdam principally because Catherine's family had lived there for generations. Albert became a partner in a sports goods business and he also represented several British firms in Holland. After the birth of their second child, a daughter called Adéle Gertrud, Albert Behar bought a large house at 40c Spengensekade, where a second daughter, Elizabeth, was born in 1925. There the family lived in upper middle-class Dutch comfort, with two housemaids, although Albert Behar was not a typical member of this class, since he made no attempt to conceal his Jewish origins. Catherine, however, brought up the children as strict Lutherans.

While Albert prospered in his business and used to visit London and Cairo on business regularly, his health deteriorated, due to his suffering from the after-effects of the phosgene or mustard gas he had experienced during the war. In the hopes that he would benefit by getting away from smoky Rotterdam, Albert took a villa at Scheveningen, a few miles from The Hague on the North Sea coast, No 4 Maastraat, near the Concert Pavilion and the Kurhaus. But the change did him little good; he developed lung cancer and finally peritonitis, the direct cause of his death at the age of forty-six, which occurred in April 1936. He left his widow comparatively well off, but before he died he made her promise to send young George to relatives in Cairo, where he had a sister married to a wealthy banker and there were several boys in the family. Accordingly the thirteen-year-old George was taken away from his school in The Hague and sent to Egypt where he was enrolled in the English School in Cairo. Another uncle, Henri Curiel, an Egyptian by birth, was a leading member of the Egyptian Communist Party, and he may well have influenced young George politically. He would return to Holland once a year for holidays, when he would stay sometimes with his mother and sisters in Scheveningen and sometimes with his uncle in Gelderland, Anthony Beijderwellen, who had no children. It was this uncle who advised George's mother after two years or so that the boy should return to Holland for good. This he did in time for Christmas 1938. Shortly afterwards he became a pupil at the Dutch High School known as MULO (*Meer Uitgebried Lager Onderwijs*) in Rotterdam. Since it was a day school, he lived with his Beijderwellen grandmother in her spacious Rotterdam house, No 35A Burgerneester Meinesz Plein.

Speaking of George, a fellow pupil, Henrik Dentro, afterwards recalled:

I think he was a very introspective boy. To us lads brought up in the strict tradition of Dutch middle-class respectability, he was a somewhat exotic figure. He had travelled widely and mixed with important people. He told us sometimes about his visits to the Pyramids and the Sphinx, the marvels of Luxor, sailing on the Nile, but he never boasted about it or bragged about his rich uncle in Cairo, or anything like that . . . We admired George and also envied him a little, because he was so good at schoolwork.

He knew several languages and often helped the other boys when they got stuck with a précis or composition . . .

He never had a close friend. I sat next to him for a long time, but we never became very close. It wasn't in George's nature to open up.

Another fellow pupil, who later went on the Rotterdam stock exchange, confirmed that George Behar knew English, French and German better than the others and that he was always willing to help them with their homework. 'Yes, it's true he kept himself to himself. Although we passed his house every day, he never asked me in and I don't think he invited any of the other classmates. In those days before the destruction of the city by the Germans, and all the post-war skyscrapers, Rotterdam was a more homely town, perhaps rather provincial, if you like. We boys used to pop into each other's places, uninvited. But none of us would have gone to George's. Perhaps we felt that we were not wanted. I think he spent most of his spare time reading. He did not join with "the gang" which went to the cinema, football matches, cycle racing. But he wasn't a softie either. He did well in gymnastics, and he was a good athlete and swimmer.' Nor could this witness understand how George ever became a traitor. 'He was the most decent boy in our class. I do not remember him ever telling a lie.'

On 28 April 1940 George saw his mother and sisters for the last time in Holland when there was a family reunion at his grandmother's home in Rotterdam to celebrate the old lady's birthday. Mrs Catherine Behar and the two girls returned to Scheveningen and they were there ten days later, on 10 May, when the Germans invaded the Low Countries. A British friend, Commander D. W. Child, who was an intelligence officer, advised her to go immediately with Adéle and Elizabeth to the Hook of Holland, where three British destroyers had arrived to evacuate the Dutch royal family and any British families in Holland who could be accommodated. George had previously begged his mother to be allowed to stay in Rotterdam to complete his studies and she consented, while his uncle, Anthony Beijderwellen, who was in the grain trade, undertook to look after him.

Catherine Behar and the two girls reached the Hook safely and embarked on one of the destroyers. All three destroyers were bombed during the voyage and only two reached Harwich safely. The third was so severely damaged that she sank *en route*. Meanwhile young George Behar was fortunate to survive the heavy bombardment and total destruction on 14 May of much of Rotterdam, which killed some 30,000 inhabitants, although Dutch resistance to the German invasion had ceased.

'It was a fearful sight,' George recalled. 'The town burned and smoked for days afterwards. The children's cries continued unceasingly. Mothers and old people crawled on their knees in the ruins, searching amid the wreckage for pots and pans and pieces of clothing. The little old street of Botersloot was completely destroyed.'

George was still living with his Beijderwellen grandmother in Rotterdam, when, shortly after the bombing, the Gestapo arrived and a neighbour who was a Dutch Nazi denounced George as a *Britischer*. He was, of course, technically at least a British subject, since his father was British by naturalization, although he had been born in Holland. At all events George was arrested by the Gestapo and taken to the concentration camp, previously a Dutch military camp, at Schoorl, near Alkmaar, about twenty miles north of Amsterdam. There, after a lengthy search by his uncle Anthony, the grain merchant, he was traced. 'Since when do the Germans make war on children?' Anthony Beijderwellen asked the camp commandant. 'I have come to collect my nephew.' But the commandant just laughed and refused to release George. However, although the camp was strongly guarded by SS troops, George managed to escape, exactly how is not known, and on 16 October 1940 he succeeded in making his way to his uncle's house at Warneveld near Zutphen in Gelderland. His uncle hid him for a short time, but then moved him to a farm nearby called The Cow's Tail (*De Koestered*) where the farmer Boer Weenink let him work on the farm and also study theology with the local pastor, since George thought of going into the Lutheran church. But after a while he discarded his theological books and decided to join the Dutch Resistance.

This worried his uncle considerably, since if he were caught by the Nazis he would certainly have been executed. But George was determined, and changing his name to Max Van Vries, he continued to work for the farmer, at the same time joining the local Resistance movement which was not very strong. Early in 1941 he heard that there was a much stronger Resistance movement based in Limburg, about eighty miles south of The Cow's Tail. Despite the fact that there was now a price on his head, he reached Limburg undetected and found an increasingly strong Resistance organization recruited from the disbanded Dutch army, navy and gendarmerie. George joined it to find that it was co-operating closely with the Dutch government in exile in London, as well as MI6 and SOE, the Special Operations Executive with headquarters in Baker Street, specializing in sabotage in enemy-occupied countries.

At first the Germans, led by the Gauleiter Arthur von Seyss-Inquart, were 'correct' in their relations with the Dutch population whom they described as their 'cousins'. But the Dutch did not relish this assumed relationship. In retaliation for the parachuting of Dutch agents by the SOE into Holland and their sabotage activities with the Resistance, the local Nazis arrested Dutch civilians at random and executed them, at the same time making the Dutch economy subservient to the German, and requisitioning thousands of tonnes of foodstuffs which resulted in strict rationing. Then a Dutch Nazi was instrumental in betraying several SOE officers and acquiring a number of SOE radio stations intact. This is not the place to relate the tragic story which followed, since it has been recorded elsewhere. As a result, fifty-four SOE agents dropped by parachute were captured, and of these forty-seven were subsequently put to death in the Mauthausen concentration camp. Meanwhile German fake messages were sent by the radio stations to London, and this ploy continued for three years before the people in Baker Street tumbled to it. From the Allied point of view it was one of the worst catastrophes of the war, and afterwards a committee of inquiry set up by the Netherlands Parliament rightly censured those in charge of the Dutch section of SOE in Baker Street for their 'grave mistakes caused by lack of experience, utter inefficiency and the disregard of the elementary rules of security'.

During this period George carried out several dangerous missions usually as a courier, sometimes cycling forty miles through the night. Eventually, however, in spite of his relatively junior role in the Resistance, he realized that something was wrong. He got in touch with his old naval intelligence friend Commander Child, who was still in Holland. Child warned him that the Gestapo were searching for Max Van Vries and advised George to get out of the country without delay. He indicated the SOE escape routes through Belgium, France and Spain to Gibraltar, which he advised him to follow, using 'safe houses' on the way, of which Child supplied him with the addresses. George took this advice and with some money he had from his uncle Anthony he bought a bicycle. At this time he disguised himself as a Trappist monk with a brown habit he obtained from a Catholic priest whom he had met in the Resistance, becoming Father Peter from the St Servatius monastery in Maastricht, the Limburg capital. A monk on a bicycle was a common sight in the Catholic south Netherlands and he passed through the frontier town of Breda in North Brabant into Belgium. In Brussels he stayed in the 'safe house' run by the legendary Belgian doctor Albert Guèrisse, known in London as Pat O'Leary, who ran a highly successful escape organization for prisoners-of-war, Allied airmen who had been shot down, and secret agents.

Crossing the French frontier safely, he was stopped by the Field Police near Lille and told he would be taken to the nearest police station for an identity check. But just as he was being bundled into a car there was an air-raid warning and in the resulting confusion Father Peter made a getaway. In Lille he found a secure hiding place by simply knocking on the door of a house and asking for refuge. The householder happened to belong to the French Resistance and provided him with a forged travel document. In Paris and Lyons he was accommodated in reliable 'safe houses' and he eventually reached Perpignan, whence he and some other escapers who had joined him were smuggled into Spain. After being interned for some time in the concentration camp at Miranda de Ebro, George was allowed to write to the British embassy in Madrid with the result that he was allowed to proceed to Gibraltar, where after intensive interrogation by a security officer, he was transported by ship to England.

In Britain he was taken to the Patriotic School at Wandsworth, then the interrogation centre for escapers and refugees from German-occupied and neutral countries. Here he was able finally to establish his bona fides, though he was disappointed that his interrogators had not heard of his work for the Dutch Resistance. On his release he went to see the Dutch secret service in London, where he was told that being a British subject he should apply to the War Office, which might put him into intelligence or SOE. But he had no luck with the War Office, where he applied for an intelligence post, so he went to stay for a time with his mother and sisters who were living near High Wycombe.

Returning to London, he happened to meet his old friend Commander Child, who had also succeeded in escaping from Holland. Child advised him to volunteer for the Royal Navy. He did so, and a few days before his twenty-first birthday, in November 1943, he became an ordinary seaman, not exactly the position he had envisaged for himself with his experience and qualifications on his arrival in England. He was sent to Portsmouth, and after a brief training ashore he was posted to a minesweeper. Some months later, his superiors discovered that he was fluent in three languages – English, Dutch and French – and that he also had a good knowledge of German.

Accordingly he was recommended for a commission and sent on an officers' training course in HMS *King Alfred* at Hove. In the spring of 1944, he passed out with excellent marks and was appointed a sub-lieutenant in the Royal Naval Volunteer Reserve, popularly known as the 'Wavy Navy'. Meanwhile like his mother and sisters, he had changed his surname by deed poll from Behar to Blake in November 1943.

4

The newly commissioned Sub-Lieutenant again applied for intelligence work but instead was sent on a submarine training course at

Portsmouth. The naval authorities may have had some intention to send him to occupied Europe in a submarine, but he found the training uncongenial and he complained to a naval surgeon that his hearing was adversely affected by the deep-water tests which he was obliged to undergo – on one occasion he fainted. So he asked for another posting, not with submarines. In the result he was posted to naval intelligence and went on a parachute course. Eventually he was seconded by the RNVR to the Dutch section of the SOE. Here he found that the section heads who were so terribly hoodwinked by the *England Spiel* disasters had been replaced by an astute organizer, Major Dobson, who was co-operating cordially with the Dutch secret service and had succeeded to a considerable extent in compensating for the tragic work of his predecessors.

'We had close linking with the Dutch Secret Service,' he later recalled. 'The work was pretty elementary, but the results often exceeded all our expectations. I would receive coded telegrams indicating the day and hour of some particular event, such as the whereabouts of a high-ranking Nazi general on Dutch territory. I would decipher these and hand them over to the co-ordinating staff for action.'

However, George Blake did not stay for long in Baker Street. In May 1944, he was posted as an interpreter to the newly formed Supreme Headquarters Allied Expeditionary Force (SHAEF) in Bushey Park and a little later to the Allied Naval Expeditionary Force (ANCXF) headquarters under Admiral Bertram Ramsey near Portsmouth. He also worked at Norfolk House in London, the headquarters of the Allied invasion chiefs – Eisenhower, Montgomery, Bradley, Ramsey, Leigh-Mallory and Bedell Smith. Blake's job was to translate and interpret German documents captured by British agents as well as those of the American OSS in German-occupied Europe. He was also detailed to conduct interrogations of captured German prisoners on the French coast after D-Day. He did his job well, although he was only one of approximately eleven hundred officers who constituted SHAEF.

George Blake landed on the Continent in the middle of 1944. In April 1945 he was at Montgomery's headquarters. On 4 May he was present at the surrender of the German North-West Army Corps –

over one million men – at Montgomery's headquarters on Luneberg Heath. Three days later the fighting was over, and Blake, now promoted to the rank of a full lieutenant, was posted as an intelligence officer to HMS *Albert*, at Hamburg. At the same time, for his services with the Dutch Resistance and the Dutch secret service, Queen Wilhelmina of the Netherlands awarded him the Cross of the Order of Nassau, Fourth Class, corresponding to the British MBE.

In Hamburg Lieutenant George Blake RNVR was put in charge of his own intelligence unit and he installed himself in an office in the large building in the Flottbeker Chausse in the docks, which had been the headquarters of Grand Admiral Doenitz, who had commanded the German navy and been nominated by Hitler as his successor after the Fuehrer's death. Blake's top priority was the collection of as much information as possible relating to the Nazi submarine service and the war at sea generally for use in the forthcoming war crimes trials. Blake and his assistants set to work with a will and Blake himself interrogated all the important U-boat and frigate commanders, whose vessels had sunk tens of thousands of tonnes of British merchant shipping.

From his office in Hamburg, working zealously for long hours, Blake turned out a mass of reports and memoranda. His German was now perfect and he did not hesitate to exert his authority when the Germans whom he interrogated continued to give the Nazi salute and *Heil Hitler*, a practice to which he put a stop. He also reported on Russian Communist infiltration, and would go to the port of Lubeck disguised as a 'displaced person' to collect evidence of Soviet propaganda, since the Russian zone frontier was only a few miles to the east. In Hamburg he also began to have Russian language lessons. He reported at length on Soviet activities in the British, French and American zones of occupation, and also in the Russian zone, where, according to his own account, he was instructed to collect information on Soviet troop movements with a view to Soviet officers being persuaded to work for British intelligence.

One day when he was in his Hamburg flat he received a call from a high-ranking officer in MI6 (SIS), Commander Kenneth Cohen RN, who on a routine visit to Hamburg wished to ascertain details of Blake's work. He noticed a tattered Russian grammar on Blake's bedside table. 'So you're learning Russian?' Cohen asked with an air of interest. 'Congratulations. But you're doing it on your own?' When Blake nodded an affirmative, Cohen remarked, 'That's not the way to do it at all.' Nothing further was said on this subject but it was to have an interesting sequel. At the same time Blake's colleagues and subordinates, many of whom were older, resented his implication that he was a professional intelligence officer while they were only amateurs. He had no time for girls or any of the other frivolities in which his fellow officers indulged. Like the black market, prostitution flourished in Hamburg. 'We have a job to do,' was his reaction to the suggestion that he should visit the red-light district in the Rieperbahn. 'I have no time for women here, anyway not for women of that kind.'

His turn for home leave came in 1947 and coincided with the Allies' decision to grant a measure of self-government to the areas of Germany which they occupied including Berlin. By this time George had become tired of or disillusioned with naval intelligence and yearned for a change, preferably to secret intelligence. His superiors in Hamburg sent a laudatory account of his activities to Major-General Gerald Templer who had been Director of Military Government in Germany and was now Director of Military Intelligence at the War Office in the hopes that he would be given another job in England and not return to Hamburg.

He got little satisfaction at the War Office, being passed from one officer or department to another and eventually given the impression that there was nothing doing in that sphere. Disappointed and discontented, he went down to Chalfont St Peter in Buckinghamshire to stay with his mother who was living there. Then, to his delight, a summons came to an interview at the Foreign Office. There he was received in a friendly manner by Kenneth Cohen, the MI6 officer who had met him in Hamburg, and they discussed his wish to go on with his Russian language lessons. He was told that in this event there was a good chance that he would be employed in foreign affairs. Meanwhile he was to apply for demobilization from the RNVR, after which he would be given a service scholarship to Cambridge where he would enrol at Downing College for a 'crash' course in Russian, after which he would be posted to the consular branch of the Foreign Office.

He thereupon was demobilized and given the gratuity which he had earned in the Navy and which he was able to add to his scholarship money. He arrived at Cambridge in October 1947, but he did not take lodgings in the university town. He rented a room in the nearby village of Madingley, from where he would cycle every morning to Downing for his lessons, where his tutors were greatly impressed by his assiduity. 'Learning Russian meant that I became acquainted with its wonderful literature,' he said afterwards. 'I also learnt more about the Soviet people and how much they had suffered during the war years.' In three months he would read Maxim Gorky's *Childhood* in the original as well as Lenin's classic political treatise *What Is To Be Done?* He did not participate in any undergraduate activities or join any clubs or societies. Nor, as in Hamburg, did he indulge in any womanizing.

By the end of the Easter term in 1948, he was declared proficient in Russian and told to report back to the Foreign Office. On doing so he was seen by the Establishment Officer who informed him that he would be joining Branch A grade IX in the Foreign Service with the temporary rank of Vice-Consul; this would serve as cover for his work as a secret agent of MI6, of which Major-General Sir Stewart Menzies was then the head. Somewhat to his surprise he was also told that he would be attached to the Far Eastern Department and in due course would be posted overseas. His appointment was dated 1 September 1948 and was subsequently published in the Annual Foreign Office List, a copy of which he proudly sent his mother as well as his uncle Anthony Beijderwellen who had survived the German occupation of Holland. In the meantime, pending his overseas posting he was attached to A 2, the Dutch section of MI6.

An embarrassing incident occurred while George Blake was working in the Dutch section, which may conceivably have affected his subsequent behaviour. One of the secretaries was Miss Iris Peake, the twenty-four-year-old daughter of the Rt Hon Osbert Peake, Member of Parliament for North Leeds and a former Financial Secretary to the Treasury, later created Viscount Ingleby. Blake was strongly attracted by her, becoming obsessed to the point of infatuation. He contrived to get himself invited to spend a week-end at Snilesworth, the Peake family's country home near Northallerton in Yorkshire. When he was there Osbert Peake, who suspected that there was something between Blake and his daughter, took Blake aside one evening after dinner and made it clear that there was absolutely no question of Blake marrying his daughter or even contemplating it. Blake was very upset by these remarks which he wrongly attributed to his host's anti-Semitism. It never occurred to him that an alliance with a member of such a blue-blooded family as the Peakes – Iris's mother was a daughter of the Earl of Essex – might be regarded as 'unsuitable' in the circumstances. At all events Blake was deeply offended and he never forgot it. In the event Miss Peake left the service shortly afterwards and became a lady-in-waiting to Princess Margaret.

A few months later, George Blake was informed of his overseas posting to Seoul, the capital of the Republic of Korea. The British Mission consisted of a Legation, the Minister being an experienced orientalist, Captain (later Sir) Vyvyan Holt CMG, MVO, a bachelor and an enthusiastic polo player, who had previously served in Baghdad and Teheran and had been in the Intelligence Corps in India during the First World War. From the outset George Blake liked him and they got on well together, both arriving in Seoul in 1949. The only other member of the diplomatic staff was the Consul, Norman Owen.

The two leading members of the small British community with whom Blake also became friendly were the Anglican bishop, the Right Rev A. C. Cooper and the Commissioner of the Salvation Army, Herbert Lord, both of whom had lived in the country and knew it and its language well. The bishop's house was just over the wall from the British Legation and Bishop Cooper later recalled that Blake often used to drop in for a chat. 'He was a fine chap,' the bishop later recalled, 'a good Christian and a regular churchgoer.' As for Commissioner Lord, he found Blake 'a very typical Foreign Office type, a man of the world, but serious-minded and rather reserved until you got to know him well. I always thought of him as a man of great self-respect and an ambitious and energetic fellow . . .'

5

For many hundreds of years Korea had been a subject kingdom of the Chinese emperors and was closed to foreigners until the Japanese invaded it during the Russo–Japanese War of 1905; they annexed it in 1910 and ruled it for the next thirty-five years. The Soviet declaration of war on Japan in August 1945 was prompted by Stalin's wish to extend Communist influence to Korea. In the following months the Americans landed troops in South Korea, stating that the purpose of the exercise was to enforce the surrender of the Japanese army, while a similar reason was given by the Russians for landing troops in the north of the country. It was agreed between the Russians and the Americans that Korea should be partitioned along the 38th parallel, the northern capital being Pyongyang and the southern Seoul, while the Allies agreed to restore Korea to full independence in five years. But this arrangement broke down when the Russians, with the help of the Chinese rebel leader Mao Tse-tung and his supporters, busied themselves in setting up a Communist regime in the north as a 'People's Republic'. The Americans retorted by appointing as President of the 'Democratic Republic' of Korea in the south Dr Syngman Rhee, an elderly, reactionary politician who had spent the war in the United States, having previously served as provisional president in secret in Seoul during the Japanese rule between the wars.

Blake also got on well with the Koreans, especially the university and art institute teachers, with whom Syngman Rhee was unpopular on account of his desire to unify the country with American support, a course of action with which the Russians and Chinese naturally disagreed. On the other hand the South Korean intelligentsia accepted America's support of Syngman Rhee as their only protection against invasion from the north, although they disliked the boisterous and promiscuous behaviour of the American army GIs. Contacts which Blake established with local liberals and socialists, who were in touch with the Communist regime in Pyongyang, indicated that the Syngman Rhee forces had advanced beyond the truce line of the 38th parallel and were even plotting to kill the North Korean

Prime Minister Kim Il-Sung. No doubt some of the accusations against Syngman Rhee were justified, but they were offset by the responsibility of the Russians and Chinese in also failing to observe the truce line by sending hundreds of Moscow trained agitators to spread subversion in South Korea.

Blake was convinced, as was Captain Holt, from information received, that the Communists in the north were planning to attack the Republic in the south. In fact the invasion began on 25 June 1950 and Seoul was occupied four days later. President Syngman Rhee and his cabinet fled from the capital to the fetid and rat-infested town of Taejon about fifteen miles south on the route to Pusan on the southern coast. The American military and political missions, consisting of some 230 individuals did likewise without informing the British Legation in Seoul of their action, which surprised and annoyed Captain Holt and his colleagues. The British Minister and his French counterpart Georges Perruche decided to remain in Seoul to protect their nationals, having every reason to believe that they would be treated as neutrals in accordance with international law. They were speedily disillusioned.

On the morning of 30 June a group of North Korean civilians, wearing red armbands to indicate that they belonged to the militia of the 'People's Republic', entered the British Legation compound. Brandishing automatic pistols they demanded that the legation cars be handed over to them. Vice-Consul Blake, accompanied by Commissioner Lord, who spoke Korean and acted as interpreter, parleyed with them, but in spite of the Vice-Consul's protests the vehicles were driven away. At the same time armed mobs were rioting, looting and burning down all the churches.

The following day, a short, stout man in the uniform of a major in the North Korean army arrived with several soldiers. He announced himself as Major Choe and demanded to see Captain Holt. He told the Minister that the Union Jack should be lowered from the legation roof because 'the sight of it might provoke the anger of the liberated people'. Captain Holt told Blake to reject this demand which Blake did. Thereupon Major Choe ordered his soldiers to climb on the roof and remove the flag. When this was done, the major neatly folded the flag and bowing politely gave it to the Vice-Consul. He added that British diplomatists would be unharmed since he was sending two sentries for their protection. The sentries in ragged uniforms with others arrived an hour later, surrounding the compound, firing their rifles in the air and demanding whisky and cigarettes. They were out of luck, since besides helping his colleagues to make a bonfire of the legation archives in the garden, Blake on his own initiative poured the contents of the legation cellar down the drain. When the sentries showed that they did not believe him, Blake took them to the drain and told them to smell. 'Whisky gone, all gone', he told them, notwithstanding which the soldiers knelt down and scooped up what remained of the Scotch in a small puddle by the drain and eagerly lapped up the dirty liquid.

Early in the morning of 2 July a van drove up to the legation gate. Blake went out as he thought the legation cars were being returned. Major Choe then appeared and told Blake and the others in the legation that they would have to come to police headquarters to have their credentials checked and they could return in twenty minutes. However, they were kept in a small room for eight hours without a meal or anything to drink before being interrogated. The Minister stated that all his official documents were in the legation, but when he was taken back there to get them, much of the building was on fire, while there were looters in the remaining rooms, throwing furniture, bed linen, kitchen utensils and anything else they could lay their hands on out of the windows. The police officer who accompanied Captain Holt said he regretted that nothing could be done to stop the looting and returned with the Minister to police headquarters.

Meanwhile Blake was being questioned, which took several hours, but he was not treated unkindly since his interrogators apparently knew all about his contacts with the local socialists. During this interrogation gun-fire could be plainly heard outside and presently a stray bullet came through the open window and lodged in the table between Blake and the commissar who was interrogating him. 'Those boys are having some fun out there,' the commissar remarked apologetically.

'Why can't we have some fun too?' asked Blake, banging his fist on the table where his action caused an inkpot to spatter its contents on the commissar's face and tunic. The commissar took it quite well, but during the pause for apologies Commissioner Lord wisely advised Blake to refrain from having more fun. At the same time Captain Holt, who maintained his composure, continued to protest against the abuse of diplomatic privilege for which his captors were responsible. But the Communists were not inclined to prolong discussion on this subject, and after several more hours the Minister and his colleagues together with the legation driver, who was a White Russian, as well as Commissioner Lord and two American business men who had also been detained, were ordered to board a truck for Pyongyang, the North Korean capital, 140 miles to the north.

When they arrived, the prisoners were put in a dilapidated school building, which they were told was an internment camp for important civilians and that they would shortly be joined by other Europeans. Only the White Russian driver was taken away and the others never saw him again, since he was almost certainly shot. At the same time the interrogations continued, this time in the presence of a Soviet official who said nothing but took copious notes. In the course of their questioning the prisoners were informed that the British and French Governments had joined the Americans 'in the war against the Korean People's Republic'. It was only some weeks later that they learned the true facts of the United Nations intervention from the French and other Europeans who had arrived in Pyongyang.

At an emergency meeting of the United Nations Security Council, at which the Soviet delegate was by some mischance absent, so that the Russians would not exercise their veto, a resolution was passed condemning the invasion and calling on an immediate cease fire and the withdrawal of the North Korean forces. This was ignored and the Communist advance continued. On 30 June President Truman authorized the use of American land, sea and air forces against the invaders, and a week later the United Nations Security Council placed the members of fifteen other nations, including the United Kingdom and Commonwealth under the US Command. President Truman appointed General Douglas Macarthur to the supreme command. However, the North Korean forces at first met with little resistance and were able to push south to the neighbourhood of Pusan where a front was eventually established.

6

At first the internees were treated fairly, and food consisting of soup, pork stew, cabbage, rice and bread, though monotonous, was not bad. On 20 July another transport arrived from the south, consisting of the French Minister and his staff, several civilians, and a large party of Catholic missionaries, headed by the Apostolic Delegate Bishop Patrick Burns, the Prefect Apostolic Monsignor Thomas Quinlan, together with other priests, Protestant deaconesses and nuns including the Mother Superior of Barefoot Carmelites who with her nuns had spent a lifetime in Korea looking after orphans and the aged. A little later they were joined by Philip Deane, the special correspondent of the London Sunday newspaper *The Observer*; he had been badly wounded with an American tank company near Taejon and taken prisoner.

George Blake was popular with his fellow internees. 'George was a good man to be interned with,' said Commissioner Lord afterwards. 'He turned his hand willingly to any kind of job, cooking, cleaning and all the other chores we had to do . . . He did it all with good humour, always ready to help others.' The French Minister also preserved his good humour, describing himself as *de-chargé d'affaires*, and when the prisoners heard on the radio, to which they were occasionally allowed to listen, that Princess Elizabeth had given birth to her daughter Princess Anne on 15 August, he opened his last bottle of vintage Burgundy and proposed a toast, which he invited the British diplomats to join, to *sa majesté, le Roi d'Angleterre, à la Princess Elizabeth et à la jeune princesse!*'

Eventually, on account of the American bombing of Pyongyang, the North Korean Communists decided to move their prisoners, whom they considered to be valuable hostages, to a safer place. On

5 September they were taken from the school to the railway station, where they saw several hundreds of wounded American GIs and officers who had been bundled into open coal trucks. The civilian internees were put into old and dirty carriages, ten to a compartment, women, priests and nuns all packed tightly together.

The journey lasted for six days and nights, with frequent long stops, due to the Americans' bombing under the impression that the train was carrying Korean troops, with arms and ammunition. An old Catholic priest and several GIs died on the way. Eventually on 11 September the train reached the town of Man-po on the Yalu river close to the border with Manchuria. The civilians were accommodated in an old building which had previously been used as Japanese customs quarantine quarters. Compared with what was to come, life for the civilian internees in Man-po was idyllic. The food was good, and Blake and others who felt like it were able to sunbathe and swim in the Yalu while the good weather lasted.

Although they were unaware of it at the time, a few days before the internees reached Man-po, American marines had landed at Inchon, the port west of Seoul, from which they launched a very successful campaign, capturing Pyongyang on 20 October. Meanwhile news of the reverse suffered by the North Korean forces reached Man-po, rations were cut and the internees were forbidden to leave the camp. They were moved to several other places and then on 26 October back to Man-po which had been heavily shelled and much of which was in ruins. It was now becoming increasingly cold and Blake and the others only had their thin summer clothes which they were wearing when they were arrested in Seoul. Nevertheless, Blake got a military tunic from a kindly Korean officer, but he gave this to an elderly nun and continued to face the bitter winds in his flannel trousers and sports jacket.

Hearing from one of the guards that the Americans had reached the Yalu nearby, Blake determined to escape. One night he crawled out of the camp and succeeded in making his way south through a forest to a valley where he imagined he would find some American advance tank patrols. Instead he encountered a North Korean Communist patrol who were doing likewise. The soldiers seized him and brought him before their captain in a nearby farmhouse.

'You are a spy,' said the officer to Blake. 'You have been caught red-handed and you will be shot immediately.' He told his men to tie Blake's hands behind his back and take him to a wall outside where he was to be executed.

As the firing squad raised their rifles, Blake shouted to the officer in Russian: 'I am not a spy. I am a civilian internee, a British diplomat. I went out of the camp at Man-po and I lost my way.'

Fortunately the officer, who had received military training in the Soviet Union, knew Russian. Blake's words had a dramatic effect. The officer dismissed the firing squad, took Blake back to the farmhouse, and invited him to share a meal of pork soup and sweet rice and gave him a packet of cigarettes. They had a long and friendly conversation about the rights and wrongs of the Korean War. Finally the officer returned Blake to the Man-po camp with his advice: 'Don't try to escape again! You haven't a chance. With your big nose and pink skin everyone will recognize you immediately as a foreigner and may take you for an American. You'll be shot if they catch you!'

Blake reached Man-po just as the North Korean authorities were preparing to despatch the internees to the north-east on foot and in what turned out to be a veritable death march. It is unnecessary to describe the details. Suffice it to state that by the time the civilian internees and the American prisoners-of-war had reached Hadjang camp about the middle of November in temperatures of between 50 and 70 degrees celsius below zero, 460 out of 780 Americans died and the fatal casualties among the civilians were in about the same proportion. Some of the Americans were deliberately shot for failing to keep up with the column, and others, Americans and internees alike, were left to die by the roadside. Blake stood up to these hardships pretty well, though he had bouts of dysentery and influenza and like everyone else suffered from frostbite. Vyvyan Holt and Norman Owen were particularly affected. 'If it were not for George Blake and Philip Deane,' the British Minister recalled later, 'I would not have survived even the last lap of the death march. At Hadjang they nursed me and Consul Owen, and they gave us their rations, although they were themselves sick and hungry.'

Indoctrination or Communist brain-washing began at Hadjang

and was intensified when the authorities, owing to the rising death rate, moved the important internees to a farmhouse at a village called Moo-Yong-Nee near Man-po. At the latter place Blake met the officer Choe, now promoted to Lieutenant-Colonel, who had arrested the British mission in Seoul, and the two, being Russian language speakers, became friendly, so that the North Korean officer was able to obtain quite favourable treatment for the British VIPs in the farmhouse. Another reason was that the Chinese Communist troops, euphemistically called 'volunteers', had flocked across the Manchurian border and joined the North Korean army in forcing General Macarthur's troops back below the 38th parallel. Macarthur, when joined by reinforcements, wished to mount another offensive against the north, but he was prevented from doing so by President Truman who removed him from his supreme command in April 1951 and replaced him by General Mathew Ridgway, who was ordered to begin truce negotiations with the North Koreans and the Chinese.

The North Koreans' attempts at indoctrination were not very effective and more or less broke down owing to the language difficulty. They improved in the autumn of 1951 with the arrival of a Russian expert from the Political Education Department of the Ministry of State Security (MGB), forerunner of the present KGB. His name was Gregory Kuzmitch, for some reason familiarly called Blondie by the internees. His influence soon made itself effectively felt since he spoke excellent English and his task as a brainwasher was to make as many converts to Communism as he could. He had long private sessions with Blake. It will be recalled that at his trial at the Old Bailey the first count in the indictment charged Blake with having committed his first offence under the Official Secrets Act in November 1951. This was when he was in communication with Kuzmitch at Moo-Yong-Nee. But it is difficult to see what secrets not known to the Russian and Chinese Blake could have imparted thirty-four months after his arrest unless it consisted of information about his naval intelligence work in Hamburg. Incidentally Kuzmitch subsequently defected to the US and assured the CIA that Blake had revealed very little about his work as Vice-Consul and intelligence officer in Seoul. Neither had he given any information about the training and organization of the British Secret Service (MI6) which might have been of use to the Communists at that time. On the other hand, according to Kuzmitch, he had expressed disillusionment with Western policies and had been very critical of the United Nations, and particularly the American and British intervention in Korea. This may be considered as some measure of justification of the Attorney-General's assertion at Blake's trial that his political and philosophical views had undergone a change in 1951 and that in his confession Blake had admitted that he had come to the conclusion that the Communist system was preferable to Western capitalism. At the same time in the light of the absence of specific details the charge in the first count of the indictment remains unconvincing. On the other hand, as Dame Rebecca West has suggested in her account of the Blake case in *The Meaning of Treason* (1965), he may well have become a Communist convert before 1951, possibly through the medium of his Egyptian Communist uncle Henri Curiel. However, in the present writer's view it was not until after his return to England from Korea that Blake became a fully fledged KGB agent.

On 27 November 1951 'Blondie' Kuzmitch told the prisoners that the truce negotiations were progressing well and that the war would be over by Christmas. A few days later a jovial North Korean general arrived and entertained the British and French diplomats to a sumptuous lunch. In the course of the meal he asked Captain Holt and M Perruche to write to the North Korean Prime Minister Kim Il-Sung expressing gratitude for the humane treatment they had received, doubtless with a view to their letters being used in clinching the truce negotiations.

'I assume, General,' the British Minister replied coldly, 'you want me to thank His Excellency the Prime Minister for the humane treatment which led to the deaths of my colleague Bishop Patrick Burns, the Apostolic Delegate of the Holy See . . . and all the others who died of privations, starvation and disease? My colleagues and I have been imprisoned and subjected to many inhumanities against all rules of international law and diplomatic convention and practice. Do you wish me to include the details of all this in my letter of thanks to His Excellency?'

'Please do not talk like that,' said the general. 'You are hurting my feelings. Some mistakes were made, but now we are treating you properly, I hope.' Nevertheless, the general departed without the letters.

Nor was the war over by Christmas, as Kuzmitch had predicted. The truce negotiations dragged on at Panmunjon throughout most of 1952 and eventually broke down in October over the question of repatriation of prisoners-of-war, and the fighting was resumed more savagely than before. The fact that conditions in the camp near Man-po remained tolerable was doubtless due to the renewed North Korean and Chinese successes.

It was not until the spring of 1953 that the Britons' ordeal came to an end. On 20 March Blake and the others – the Minister, Consul, Bishop Cooper, Monsignor Quinlan, Commissioner Lord and Philip Deane – were told that they would be taken to Pyongyang as a prelude to their release. They were then driven to the North Korean capital in a large lorry which had been converted into a caravan with sleeping berths. The journey took forty-three hours and on their arrival they were treated to a sumptuous meal by a North Korean brigadier, consisting of a large quantity of caviar, ham, eggs, butter and white bread. They remained in Pyongyang until 8 April, about the time that the truce negotiations were resumed, during which period they were given new clothes, shown Russian films including the incomparable Ulanova dancing at the Bolshoi ballet, and English and American magazines, from which they learned of the death of King George VI and the accession of Princess Elizabeth to the United Kingdom throne. The day before they continued on their homeward journey, they were introduced to the North Korean correspondents of the London *Daily Worker* and the French Communist *L'Humanité*. But the British gave nothing away.

'British journalists whom I met at the truce talks in Panmunjon always boasted that there is freedom in Britain,' one reporter asked Philip Deane. 'Aren't you free to talk? Or are you afraid to talk in front of your diplomats?'

'It is quite correct that there is freedom in Britain,' Captain Holt intervened. 'But the seven of us here are not free men.'

The seven members of the British party were driven to Antung, the frontier town in Manchuria, where they were put up in the best hotel and for the first time since their captivity enjoyed such luxuries as clean bed linen and scented soap in the bathrooms. Although the British Government had made its first request for the release of the British prisoners to Moscow on 16 July 1950, subsequently repeated several times, it took the North Korean authorities thirty-four months to grant it. The delay was somewhat implausibly attributed to the need to keep the prisoners under North Korean protection 'until the barbarous American bombing should stop, so that the internees could travel safely to the frontier'.

They were met at the hotel in Antung by the Second Secretary in the Soviet Embassy in Peking, an amiable individual called Vassiliev, who told them that it was his 'pleasant duty' to accompany them to Moscow, since their release had been arranged by the Soviet Government. This he did, the party travelling by train to Peking decorated with Picasso's doves of peace, and then on to the trans-Siberian express at the Sino–Soviet frontier, where they had comfortable sleeping cars.

At Moscow airport a RAF Hastings from West Berlin was waiting to take them to Gatow. After a brief rest in Berlin the seven Britons were flown to the RAF station near Abingdon in Oxfordshire, where they were greeted by senior officials of the Foreign Office, the Archbishop of Canterbury, the Salvation Army and the Irish Ambassador, Mr Frederick Boland, who welcomed Monsignor Quinlan.

They were then allowed to see the press. They were asked by some of the journalists whether the statements ascribed to them by the North Koreans, such as 'condemning the massacre of Korean women and children by American bomber aircraft', were true. This was strongly denied by Captain Holt speaking for himself and the others. 'What I said at Pyongyang,' he declared, 'was that when I came home I would do my best within the narrow limits of my possibilities to try and help to bring about a just and fair peace. I did say this quite voluntarily. My colleagues Mr Blake and Mr Owen said nothing at all.' Similar denials were made by Philip Deane and Commissioner Lord.

Why these seven men were released three months before the armistice was concluded remains a mystery. Meanwhile Blake and the other diplomats were sent on leave to recuperate. Captain Holt was knighted shortly afterwards by the Queen, although his poor health did not let him enjoy the honour for long, since he retired from the Foreign Service in 1956 and died four years later at the age of sixty-four. There was some talk of giving Blake an award, perhaps an OBE, but on account of his special position in intelligence the idea was dropped. Instead he received a letter from the Foreign Secretary, Anthony Eden, thanking him for his loyal service and sympathizing with him for his sufferings during his imprisonment.

7

After a spell of sick leave during which he stayed with his mother in her west London flat in Baron's Court and recovered his health, George Blake reported to the Foreign Office and was detailed to work in MI6 London headquarters in Broadway, Westminster, and later in a branch in Cromwell Road. The branch concerned was the Technical Operations Department, concerned with bugging and the secret opening of diplomatic bags. Eventually the two operations were split and Blake, according to his own account, was appointed Assistant Chief of the bugging department code-named Y. Among those whose quarters were bugged, according to Blake, were those of the Polish Trade Delegation in Brussels, the Commercial Attaché in the Soviet Embassy in Copenhagen, the Third Secretary of the Bulgarian Legation in London, and various individuals in Cairo. 'On the whole bugging by SIS was carried out on a large scale – they spent vast sums on it. Some of these operations were conducted in conjunction with the CIA.' It was at this period that Blake began to work for the Soviets as well as the British.

By this date the wartime and post-war head of the secret intelligence service (known as 'C'), Sir Stewart Menzies, had been succeeded by his deputy, Major-General Sir John ('Sinbad') Sinclair who like Menzies refused to believe in the spy Kim Philby's guilt. Incidentally Philby described the new 'C' as 'not overloaded with mental gifts (he never claimed them)' but 'humane, energetic and so obviously upright that it was impossible to withhold admiration', adding that 'it was distasteful to lie in my teeth to the honest Sinclair'. The SIS under Sinclair's leadership was now concentrating on the Middle East, helping among other projects to overthrow the anti-West Iranian Prime Minister Mohammed Mossadeg and bring back the exiled Shah to Teheran, as well as engaging in more dubious projects such as a plot to assassinate the Egyptian premier Nasser, which fortunately did not materialize, though it was said to have had Anthony Eden's blessing. Blake, who was already a KGB agent and passing details of these matters to the Russians, expected to be posted in due course to the Middle East. In fact his immediate destination was West Berlin where he arrived on 14 April 1955, practically two years after his return from Korea.

By this time Blake had married a pretty girl called Gillian Allan, who also worked in MI6 and in fact was his office secretary. George had left his mother's flat and had taken lodgings in All Souls' Place, Great Portland Street, possibly to facilitate his work for the KGB. Gillian's father, Colonel Arthur Allan, worked in the Foreign Office as a Russian linguistic expert, and he lived at Weybridge, where Blake used to be invited for weekends. Although he was in love with Gillian, the idea of marriage did not appeal to Blake and it was Gillian who pushed him into their engagement. By late summer 1954 Blake was told that he would be going to Berlin, although the actual posting was to be delayed until the following spring. However, under the impression that the posting was to be immediate the marriage took place in rather a hurry, the ceremony on 23 September 1954 being in the parish church, St Peter and St Thomas, in the Marylebone district where Blake lived.

The bride wore a white wedding dress, while the groom for the first time in his life donned a morning coat, in which he felt strange and uncomfortable. Since he had no close friends, George asked the bride's brother to be the best man, to which he agreed. Mrs Catherine Blake was present with her two daughters, the elder Elizabeth being married to an ex-Royal Navy officer named Wilson in Kent, and the younger Adéle being as yet unmarried. George's uncle Anthony Beijderwellen and his wife came over from Holland,

and Commander D. W. Child, who now managed a yachting holiday agency in London, was also present, as well as a spattering of officials and secretaries from MI6 and the Foreign Office. There was a reception given by the Allan family after which the young couple left to spend their honeymoon in the south of France.

Since the Berlin posting did not come through as soon as they expected, the newly-weds spent the intervening months with the bridegroom's mother, Mrs Catherine Blake, in her flat in Charleville Mansions, Baron's Court. Before leaving for Berlin, Blake was told that he would be accommodated in the SIS office in the Olympic Stadium, the scene of Nazi party rallies and now the headquarters of the British Military Commandant, Major-General R. C. Cottrell-Hill, although he would have nothing to do with the military establishment. His immediate chief was to be the nominal Foreign Office representative Peter Lunn, son of the ski champion Sir Arnold Lunn and himself no mean hand at the sport. George and Gillian Blake were allotted a five-room flat at 26 Platanen Allee in Charlottenburg, a select and pleasant residential suburb of West Berlin. The building had been taken over by the British authorities for officers and officials and was reserved for British and British-sponsored tenants.

The Blakes' flat was rather sparsely furnished and George was unwilling to buy additional furniture on the grounds that he did not know how long they would be in Berlin. Their social life was very circumscribed, and they hardly ever went to parties given by other members of the British community, keeping themselves very much to themselves, although they gave a party in their flat to celebrate the christening of their first child, a boy named Anthony after his Dutch uncle Anthony Beijderwellen who was the boy's godfather. On the other hand, George would regularly take his wife to dine in smart restaurants, such as the Maison de France in the French sector, and also to concerts since Gillian shared her husband's love of music. He would usually come home for lunch from his office in the Olympic Stadium buildings in his official Volkswagen car, no doubt to compensate for having to work late on several evenings a week.

Blake's recreations were swimming and riding, in which his wife joined him. Gillian persuaded him to buy a Ford car from a colleague who was leaving, and in this, besides shopping visits to East Berlin, they took several holidays, to Lake Garda in Italy, and St Anton in Austria, where Gillian introduced George to skiing which she had learned at her finishing school in Switzerland. They also motored via Venice to Dubrovnik in Yugoslavia as Blake, so he told his wife, was anxious to gain some first-hand knowledge of Tito's 'lilberalized' Communist regime. George's mother stayed with them several times in Charlottenburg, accompanied by her younger daughter, a shrewd young lady who was to marry a scientist working for the United Nations.

As a Member of the British House of Commons, I visited Germany on several occasions during this period and it was on one of them in the summer of 1955 that I called on Peter Lunn, who had been informed of my visit, since I had previously been an MI6 officer during the war and had asked a former colleague in Broadway for an introduction. While I was talking to him, Blake, only recently arrived, came into the room and Lunn introduced us. After Blake had left, Peter Lunn remarked what a good agent he was turning out to be. In fact, although I was not aware of it at the time, Blake had with the encouragement of his superiors become an admitted double agent, feeding his Soviet masters with fake as well as true information, while at the same time passing them as much secret material as he could glean from the official files in Lunn's office. Besides staying out late at night because, as he explained to his wife, he had to meet his 'contacts', alleged German and other agents working for him and 'the Firm' as he called the SIS, he also visited East Berlin where such consumer goods as there were there were much cheaper than in the West, a feature which attracted many British officers' wives, although they were not encouraged to make purchases in the German Democratic Republic (GDR), except for vegetables, flowers, books, newspapers, gramophone records and music sheets. The principal store was known as the KO (*Kaufhaus des Ostens*), and an assistant in this emporium where the Blakes both went shopping, may well have been used by George as a 'cut-out' for the transmission of documents and microfilms. Blake may also have used a *dybok* or secret hiding place where material of this kind could be left and afterwards collected by a KGB agent. Thus George Blake was probably speaking the truth when he stated afterwards that he never personally knew any of these KGB agents from the KGB chief Ivan Serov to his numerous subordinates, although it has been said that Serov was in the habit of visiting East Berlin and that on at least one occasion Blake met him there.

Besides supplying the Russians with the names of Germans and others working for the British, he also gave his British superiors the names of Germans working for the Russians. One of these was an attractive brunette Fraulein Ursula Schmidt, who was employed as a typist at the RAF base at Gatow and gave the Russians details about the equipment of British and American military aircraft, for which she received a monthly retainer of 1,200 DM (about £105) from the Soviets. Two other Germans who helped her were like her arrested and convicted, but they all received relatively mild sentences of under five years' imprisonment.

On the other hand Blake gave the Russians particulars of an important East German defector Lieutenant-General Robert Bialek, former Inspector-General of the East German People's Police (*Volkspolizei*) and in charge of the GDR's State Security Service (SSD). He was granted political asylum in 1953 and installed under an assumed name in a flat in the same block in the Platanen Allee where the Blakes lived. Special care was taken to protect him, his flat being fitted with automatic locks and steel window shutters in addition to an alarm system which communicated with a British security office. Nevertheless, he was always in constant fear of his life, though as a rule he never left the flat except with an official escort and his Alsatian dog. Unfortunately, one evening in February 1956, he went out for a short walk without waiting for his escort to arrive. At the corner of Platanen Allee and Leistik Strasse, two men emerged from the shadows, pounced on Bialek and bundled him into a waiting car. He had been betrayed by Blake, who had discovered his identity and informed the Russians.

Both the British Commandant in West Berlin and the British Government made repeated protests, but the Soviet authorities denied all knowledge of Bialek's whereabouts. However, it was later established that he had been taken to his old SSD headquarters in East Berlin and executed after prolonged 'interrogations'.

Perhaps Blake's chief coup in the same year was alerting the Russians to the 'discovery' of the secret underground tunnel, code-named Gold, which had been built by the Americans and extended for approximately one-third of a mile from Rudow, a suburb of the American zone of West Berlin, to Alt Gleinicke in the Soviet zone in East Berlin. The tunnel, which cost the Americans about one million dollars to construct, was full of electronic equipment, much of it of British manufacture, and was used to tap and record all the telephone communications in East Berlin, including those to the Soviet *Kommandtura* in Potsdam, as well as the cables which linked the Soviet zone with Warsaw and Moscow. Blake drew a plan of the tunnel which he handed over for delivery to the Russians. He had already given them the minutes of the top secret SIS and CIA meeting in London in December 1953 at which the operation had been jointly planned by the British SIS and the American CIA. These actions of Blake's was one of the matters described in that part of his trial at the Old Bailey which took place *in camera*. When the Russians dug down into the tunnel at Alt Gleinicke in April 1956, after it had been in use for about a year, they found no one there, but an examination of the tunnel quickly revealed its purpose. The Russians, who had, thanks to Blake, known about it for some time, made excellent propaganda of their discovery, taking about 90,000 East Berliners on well-publicized conducted tours of 'the capitalist warmongers' expensive subterranean listening post'.

An important defector besides Blake whose identity Blake disclosed to the Russians was Lieutenant-Colonel Peter Popov, a Soviet military intelligence (GRU) officer. Popov was originally stationed in Vienna, where he volunteered his services to the Americans in 1953, by the simple expedient of dropping a note on the front seat of an American diplomat's car. His services were accepted and he was assigned a CIA (Central Intelligence Agency) case officer, one George Kisvalter, who had been brought up in St Petersburg before the Revolution and spoke fluent Russian. During the next two years Popov supplied Kisvalter with the names or code-names, in some cases acronyms, of upwards of four hundred Soviet agents in the

West. In 1955 he returned to Moscow on leave and was then posted to East Berlin, since the GRU had no suspicions of his duplicity. However, his transfer meant that the CIA had no means of communicating with him. Popov also realized this with the result that he wrote a letter to Kisvalter explaining his difficulty and he handed the letter to a member of a British military mission touring East Germany. This officer passed the letter to the MI6 office in the Olympic Stadium in West Berlin where it landed on George Blake's desk with instructions to forward it to the CIA in Vienna. This Blake did but not before he had read the contents and informed the Russians who took some time to react.

Popov continued his meetings with Kisvalter, but it was not until Popov disclosed that he was sending a young girl secret agent named Tairova to New York on an American passport which belonged to a Polish-born hairdresser living in Chicago and had been 'lost' during a visit to her native Poland, that Popov definitely came under suspicion. The girl, to whose mission the FBI had been somewhat reluctantly alerted by the CIA, was subjected to such a degree of surveillance by the Bureau from the moment she landed at New York's Idlewild airport that she felt she had been 'blown' and returned to Moscow of her own accord. The GRU now recalled Popov to Moscow where he blamed Tairova for what had happened. His explanation was accepted and for the time being he continued to work as usual in GRU headquarters. At the same time he was assigned a CIA member of the US Embassy named Russell Langrelle as his American contact.

The KGB, who were keeping an eye on Popov, took action on 16 October 1959 when they arrested him on a Moscow bus in the act of passing a message to Langrelle. The CIA man was arrested at the same time, but he successfully pleaded diplomatic immunity and was released. But Popov met the fate which similar defectors had suffered in the past, having admitted (according to *Izvestia*) that he deserved 'the supreme penalty'. It took a grim form. He was thrown live into a blazing furnace in the presence of an audience of his GRU colleagues.

It was at this time that Blake made a new acquaintance of the same age who was to have fateful consequences for him. Horst

Eitner, son of a German artisan, had been a member of the Hitler Youth and a Nazi opportunist, but he had changed his coat and become a 'good German', obtaining employment in the organization of General Reinhard Gehlen, Director of West German Intelligence. Boisterous and vulgar and fond of good living yet not without ability, he was married to a Polish brunette called Brigitte who had been in a Russian labour camp. As one of Gehlen's operators in West Germany he exposed several American officers working for the Russians, but his extravagant way of life annoyed his chief who eventually fired him. Eitner then offered his services to the British, and after investigation was taken on at a reduced salary and sent to Berlin. Blake's superiors thought they might work well together and put them in touch with each other instructing Blake that he was not to meet him in his office or flat and that he must use another name. The name which Blake chose was Van Vries which he had used in Holland in his Resistance days, so that he could tell Eitner that he was a Dutchman. What Blake did not at first know was that Eitner was also working for the Russians as well as the British and like Blake was a double agent. But Blake discovered this sometime in 1958 and it worried him considerably. Thus when early in 1959 the Russians suggested to Blake that he should ask for his recall to London where they considered that he might be more useful to them in MI6 headquarters, Blake was only too glad to accede to their request. This was granted since Blake had been nearly four years in Berlin and was felt to be justified in asking for a change.

Accordingly, in April 1959, the Blakes returned to London. Gillian Blake was expecting their second child, who turned out to be another boy; he was born shortly afterwards and called James. George rented a furnished flat in a semi-detached house at Bickley, sixteen miles south-east of London in Kent. Meanwhile he resumed his work at MI6 headquarters. Dressed in a dark suit and carrying a rolled umbrella which he was in the habit of losing, he travelled to Victoria by the 9.14 am train arriving shortly before ten at his office and leaving by the 6.24 train from Victoria so as to be home by seven. However, as it later transpired, he sometimes took a slightly earlier train, the 6.18 to Bromley South, where he would meet a Soviet contact for a few minutes, handing over microfilm inside a folded newspaper, an action likely to pass unnoticed in the rush hour. He would then catch another train, which went to Bickley, the next station, only a couple of miles away, so that he could arrive home at the usual time.

It had long been the intention of the authorities in Broadway to send Blake to the Middle East, an area in which the Soviet Union was becoming increasingly interested. First, Blake had to become fluent in Arabic or at least acquire a practical knowledge of the language. The Suez crisis, and the ill-fated British invasion of Egypt following Nasser's seizure of the canal in the summer of 1958, emphasized Britain's need for more Arab linguists if she were to maintain any worthwhile influence in such Arab-speaking states as Jordan, Kuwait and other countries in the Persian Gulf. Accordingly Blake was sent to the Middle East College for Arabic Studies (MECAS), founded many years before in Jerusalem when Palestine was under British mandate. After the creation of the state of Israel, it was moved to pro-British Lebanon, where it was housed at Shemlan, a village in the hills above Beirut. MECAS primarily served the needs of the Foreign Office, but British industrial and trading companies in the Middle East could also make use of it for the instruction of their employees in Arabic.

George and Gillian Blake arrived in Beirut with their two sons, Anthony and the baby James, in September 1960, but they did not stay in the school buildings with their class rooms and dormitories, but lived in a house on the edge of the village which George rented for £350 a year, which he could easily afford since in addition to his student's allowance of £100 a month he continued to draw his salary as a member of the SIS.

The course normally lasted eighteen months, but George Blake's progress was so rapid, helped perhaps by what he had picked up of the language as a boy in Egypt, that the Principal of MECAS recommended that he should be sufficiently proficient in Arabic at the end of nine or at the most ten months. But, as events turned out, he was not destined to complete this abbreviated course.

In the same month as the Blakes arrived in the Lebanon, Horst Eitner, who was still operating in Berlin, was discovered by Federal Germany's secret service, 'acting on information received', to be a double agent working for the Russians. In fact he was denounced by his wife Brigitte, who was jealous on account of his association with another woman. After being shadowed for several weeks by Gehlen's men, he was arrested and charged with communicating intelligence to a potential enemy. While in prison, awaiting trial, he wrote to Blake for help but received no reply, since his letter was addressed to Van Vries. Bitter and disillusioned, he then told the interrogating judge that he had become a double agent at British instigation, specifically identifying Van Vries as being responsible. Eitner's trial and imprisonment by the West Germans followed, but the information about Blake which was communicated by the Federal authorities to the British was at first disbelieved, since it was thought that Eitner had falsely denounced Blake out of spite. However, Blake's treachery was unexpectedly confirmed by an important Communist defector, Colonel Michael Golienewski, who had been head of the Polish Military Intelligence organization in East Berlin and gone over to the Americans. Golienewski positively identified Blake as being a Soviet spy, and also the members of the Portland Spy Ring already mentioned. His information was forwarded by the State Department to London, followed by Golienewski himself, who was closely questioned by the British security authorities, including Sir Dick White, the former head of MI5 who had succeeded 'Sinbad' Sinclair as SIS chief in Broadway.[1] The British security and intelligence authorities reluctantly concluded that Blake was a traitor, and the Prime Minister, then Harold Macmillan, was told. In the event it was agreed that Blake should if possible be brought back from Lebanon to face the charge of treachery.

So as not to arouse suspicions, since he could easily have taken

[1] Sinclair was dismissed for bungling an attempt to get up-to-date information on Soviet warships during the visit of the Russian leaders Khruschev and Bulganin to England in 1956, by sending frogman Commander L. P. K. ('Buster') Crabb, to attach a limpet device to one of the escorting vessels. The Russians, who observed Crabb's activities, protested to the Eden Government which embarrassingly apologized, causing a parliamentary storm. Crabb's headless body was subsequently recovered by fishermen, after the pages of the register of the Portsmouth hotel, where Crabb had stayed the night before his foray with a companion, were torn out on MI6 orders.

refuge in pro-Soviet Syria, a telegram was sent to Blake from the Foreign Office through Nicholas Elliott, the MI6 station head in Beirut, requesting his presence in London 'for important consultations'; but there was no suggestion of immediate urgency. After telling his wife that he might be wanted for a new posting or even promotion, he replied that he would leave by air on Easter Monday, 3 April 1961. On Easter Sunday afternoon he asked a few friends from MECAS and the British Council to his house for drinks, telling them that he had been invited to London on business and that he expected to go back to Shemlan by the following Saturday in time for his son Anthony's birthday. He then took off from Beirut airport as arranged, arriving in London on Easter Monday afternoon and spending the night with his mother at her house in Radlett.

2

Prison and Escape

I

BLAKE reported at Broadway on Easter Tuesday morning and was taken up to Sir Dick White's office on the sixth floor. With Sir Dick were Terence Lecky and another MI6 officer, Harold Shergold, who were to act as interrogators. Blake was told that he would have to answer their questions, since there was evidence that he had committed offences under the Official Secrets Act and this must be investigated. Lecky and his colleague thereupon directly accused Blake of being a Soviet agent. Blake at first denied everything on which he was questioned, asking to be allowed to make a full report which, he said, 'would explain everything'. Sir Dick told him that he would have an opportunity of doing so but that the questioning must continue. Eventually the interrogators broke off for lunch and Blake went out to have something to eat, after he had been told to return in an hour or so. When he left the building Blake was trailed by two Special Branch police officers, who watched Blake approaching a telephone kiosk as if to make a call and then suddenly changing his mind. He appeared to be in some distress since he repeated the performance, the assumption being that he thought of telephoning his local Soviet contact for advice but could not make up his mind.[1] Blake's actions were reported by the detectives to

[1] The contact was a GRU officer, Nikolai Karpekov, who ranked as a Counsellor in the Soviet Embassy. Also there was a reference to him in Blake's black notebook containing lists of names with their telephone numbers alongside. Karpekov appeared as Nikki and his telephone number as Kensington 8955.

Broadway, so that when his interrogation was resumed the fact of his indecision was noted in evidence against him. Eventually he broke down and confessed to the charges of treachery and signed a statement to this effect. Yet it was a matter of touch-and-go for the interrogators. 'Blake broke at a time when there was hardly another question to ask him,' remarked a CIA officer who was told the story. 'If Blake had held out, they would not have had a case.' To which the intelligence expert Kenneth de Courcy, who was in prison with Blake, has added: 'They couldn't have got Blake if they hadn't got him to confess. A confession is almost essential unless you catch the chap red-handed at a drop!' Immediately after Blake had signed his confession Detective Superintendent Louis Gale and Detective Chief-Inspector Ferguson Smith appeared and were shown the written confession, upon which they arrested him and drove him to Bow Street police station where he was formally charged. Afterwards, in the late afternoon, he was brought before the Chief Metropolitan Magistrate Sir Robert Blundell, who having heard the charges remanded the prisoner in custody at Brixton until 22 April.

Meanwhile Gillian Blake had received a message from the British Embassy in Beirut that her husband had been detained in London, but she was surprised to hear nothing from him, not even a greetings telegram for Anthony's birthday on 10 April. Two days later a woman from the Foreign Office arrived at the Blakes' villa in Shemlan and broke the news as tactfully as she could that George was in custody accused of serious offences. Furthermore the visitor told her that she must pack up their belongings and fly with her and the two children to London next day, seats already having been booked for them. Their flight duly took place and on arrival in London Gillian Blake was advised not to stay there, so as to avoid news reporters. Consequently she went down to Sussex and stayed with friends. She was now pregnant with her third child which was expected to be born during the next couple of months.

While George was on remand she was allowed to see him in Brixton which she did. But it must have been a distinctly painful reunion in the presence of a prison or security officer. When he came up before the Chief Magistrate on 22 April, George Blake was committed for trial at the Old Bailey, while the magistrate issued the brief notice to the press which has already been mentioned.

After his trial and conviction Blake was taken to Wormwood Scrubs prison in north London, which had been constructed in the previous century by the head of the Prison Commission Sir Edmund du Cane and was the first institution of its kind with the 'separate block' system considered an improvement on the 'radial' plan in use in the older prisons like Pentonville, but retaining such features as cellular confinement and 'hard labour'. During the intervening years hard labour such as the treadmill and the crank had been abolished and remission of sentence for good conduct introduced. On arrival at Wormwood Scrubs prisoners were at first usually kept under observation in the prison hospital, particularly necessary in Blake's case since he had suffered something in the nature of a nervous breakdown to which his incredibly long sentence had no doubt contributed.

In Blake's time Wormwood Scrubs, in accordance with du Cane's plan, comprised four large oblong cell blocks or 'halls', as they were called, built parallel to each other, with workshops and other buildings such as the chapel and the exercise yards between them, the whole surrounded by a twenty-foot wall. The halls, known by the first four letters of the alphabet, were identical in size with four landings or 'galleries' with the doors to the cells. At each corner there was a turret consisting of a small room, used as an office by the gallery officer and for other purposes. For instance, the inmate responsible for the production of the prison magazine had an office in one of these turrets.

Blake was initially put on what was known as 'special watch', treatment reserved for prisoners who had attempted to escape, or were considered likely to do so. A 'special watch' prisoner was allocated a special security cell in C Hall, which did not have a ventilating shaft under the floor in case he should use it as a getaway: there was a light in his cell kept on throughout the night; and all his clothes except for a shirt and slippers had to be placed outside the cell at night. In the daytime he had to wear coloured patches of cloth, orange, red and yellow, on each item of his outer clothing. At the same time his cell was searched regularly and he was not allowed to take part in most communal activities.

Blake was subjected to these experiences for several months, during which period he was visited by MI6 officers who debriefed him. He also had visits from his mother and Gillian, who had given birth to a third son, christened George Patrick. Towards the end of September, the Director-General of the Security Service, Sir Roger Hollis (later suspected himself of being a Soviet agent) told the prison Governor, Mr T. W. H. Hayes, that Blake's debriefing was coming to an end, and asked the Prison Commissioners to transfer him to Winson Green Prison in Birmingham. However, the only result was that Blake ceased to be a 'special watch' prisoner and was placed in an ordinary cell on the ground floor of D Hall. The Prison Commissioners declined to move Blake to Birmingham on the ground that it would be a considerable hardship to his wife and mother to visit him if he were so far away from London. In February 1962, it was also ruled unnecessary to have a security officer as well as a prison warder present at these family meetings since both Mrs Catherine Blake and Mrs Gillian Blake were regarded as completely trustworthy and most unlikely to pass the prisoner surreptitious messages or forbidden articles. Meanwhile Blake was allowed to take a correspondence course in Arabic, although he was not allowed to go to educational classes held in other blocks, since prisoners in D Hall had to be accompanied by a warder, and there were not enough warders available to escort Blake and the other prisoners in his block to these classes.

There were four prisoners, in particular, who had cells in D Hall and with whom Blake was to become friendly. Two were convicted spies, one Russian and the other English, the third was an English expert on the subject of intelligence, and the fourth was an Irishman, who was serving a sentence for attempting to commit 'grievous bodily harm'. Their names were Gordon Lonsdale, William John Vassall, Kenneth de Courcy, and Seán Bourke.

Gordon Arnold Lonsdale, whose real name was Konon Trofimovich Molody, had entered Great Britain on a Canadian passport, and he always claimed to be a Canadian of East European descent. In fact he was a thirty-nine-year old Russian, who had been born in the Soviet Union, the son of a well-known scientist. After serving with the Red Army in the war, he joined the KGB, and in order to acquire a Canadian accent, he spent some time in Canada where he applied for and successfully obtained a Canadian passport in the name of a man who had died. Although he was married and had a wife and son in Moscow, in London he posed as a playboy and had quite a success with the girls, living in a smart apartment in the White House, near Regent's Park. In the line of duty he masterminded the so-called Portland Spy Ring designed to collect information on nuclear submarines. This he did by pretending to be the Assistant Naval Attaché in the US Embassy and getting his information from an old naval petty officer named Harry Houghton, working as a clerk in the Admiralty, and his mistress Ethel ('Bunty') Gee. Communications were made through two other KGB operatives, Peter Kroger, an antiquarian book dealer (who specialized in works on sado-masochism and torture) and his wife Helen, whose real names were Morris and Lorna Cohen, a Jewish couple who came from New York. The spy ring was exposed by Houghton's bungling which put MI5 on the trail, with the result that they were arrested and brought to trial at the Old Bailey in March 1961, a few weeks before Blake stood in the same dock before the same judge, Lord Parker. The five defendants, who all pleaded not guilty, were all convicted of espionage after a six-day trial. Lonsdale, whom the Lord Chief Justice branded a 'professional spy', was sentenced to twenty-five years, the Krogers each getting twenty years and Houghton and Bunty Gee fifteen. 'It is a dangerous career,' the judge told Lonsdale in sentencing him, 'and one in which you must be prepared, as you no doubt are, to suffer, if and when you are caught.'

Lonsdale and Blake were supposed to be kept separate from each other and not allowed to converse. Henry Brooke, the Home Secretary at this time, assured the House of Commons more than once that this was so. In fact, it was not. Blake and Lonsdale frequently saw each other and would converse in Russian in a low voice, Blake doing most of the talking. Questioned by a *Sunday Times* reporter, Lonsdale said he liked Blake. 'I learned a lot from him,' he added. No doubt Lonsdale reported these conversations when he got back to Moscow, since he served only three years of his twenty-five-year sentence. In April 1964, he was removed from Wormwood Scrubs, taken to Berlin as the result of an Anglo–Russian spy exchange deal, and exchanged at the Heertstrasse checkpoint for the British business man Greville Wynne, who had been sentenced to eight years for espionage in the previous year, while his Soviet contact Oleg Penkovsky was convicted of treason and executed. No doubt the Russians had the best of this deal.[1]

2

William John Vassall, the son of a Church of England clergyman, was a homosexual, who while working in the Naval Attaché's office in the British Embassy in Moscow, was blackmailed as the result of a compromising encounter which had been engineered by the KGB in 1955. He became a spy and carried on with his work after he returned to the Admiralty, continuing except for a short break after the Portland case, when he was advised to 'lie low', until his arrest in 1962. Like Blake he pleaded guilty at his trial, and he was sentenced to eighteen years on 5 November 1962. After nine months as a 'special watch' prisoner, Vassall saw a good deal of Blake, when they used to talk in the exercise yard. They had both worked for the Russians with the difference that Vassall had been blackmailed. 'You were one of the victims,' Blake told him, 'and what happened to you was one of the recognized methods used by intelligence or security services throughout the world.' Blake also asked him about the Catholic church and supposed it was a great help to him, which Vassall agreed it was. According to Vassall, Blake added that in early life he had thought of becoming a Roman Catholic priest but 'decided that the alternative course of the Communist world was the solution for him'. He asked if he could borrow a large volume

---

[1] In October 1970 a brief announcement was made in Moscow to the effect that K. T. Molody, who had been awarded two high decorations, the Red Star and the Red Banner, had died of a heart attack while picking mushrooms. He was forty-eight.

of the lives of the Catholic saints which had been sent to Vassall and which Vassall was glad to lend him. Vassall subsequently asked Blake which saint he particularly liked or admired, and he replied without hesitation 'St John of the Cross'. The choice of this Spanish mystic Carmelite priest, who died in 1591, is interesting, due perhaps to Arthur Symons's translation of his verses as *Images of Good and Evil*. While Blake was still at Wormwood Scrubs, Vassall, for some inexplicable reason, was moved to Maidstone.

Kenneth Hugh de Courcy, titular Duke de Grantmesnil, was convicted of fraud – framed, as he alleges – at the Old Bailey in December 1963, in which month he arrived at Wormwood Scrubs. Six months later he escaped but was almost immediately recaptured, having been betrayed by a woman friend in whom he had unwisely confided. 'I should explain,' he wrote in a long unpublished memorandum composed in prison, 'that I escaped in order to force open the new evidence in my own case which I knew to exist and to demonstrate thereby that my trial was wholly based upon fraudulent evidence devised and fabricated for the purpose of reducing me to silence and that it was done with political motives which also suited non-political interests.'

After his recapture de Courcy was put on 'special watch' in C Hall, but in March 1965 he was taken off this treatment and transferred to D Hall where he saw a lot of Blake. Of course his name was not unknown to Blake since he knew of de Courcy when de Courcy was running the *Intelligence Digest*, copies of which Blake had sent to Moscow. Nevertheless, the two became firm friends in spite of their political differences, and Blake got all the information he could from de Courcy about his case. 'In those days,' wrote de Courcy, 'the D Hall cells were open all day from 7.30 am to 8 pm. We therefore spent almost our entire free time together in one way or another from March 1965 to October 1966. We also met during working hours for half an hour's relaxation fairly often. During all the time Blake took considerable trouble to read most of the papers in my case and became quite a master of its far-reaching issues.'

Although not himself a homosexual, Blake (according to de Courcy) 'took a lively interest in their doings, as he did in all sexual matters of any kind. Blake took advantage of Vassall's homosexual advances and pumped that young man bone dry. He extracted from him a full list of everyone in high places who indulged in sexual perversions.' De Courcy's estimate of Blake's character in other respects is not without interest. 'He was really three quite separate personalities,' de Courcy wrote in the memorandum of his prison experiences already mentioned. 'One was charming, witty, good natured and kind. The second was despairing, pessimistic, defeatist, while the third man was cruel, ruthless and without regard to personal or any other loyalty.[1] When that third man bared his teeth (which he physically in fact did), a sensible person could see that he was an extremely dangerous customer. His eyes spoke of Blake No 1: his weak face of Blake No 2 and his hands of Blake No 3. They are as cruel hands as ever I saw. I myself always hoped that No 1 would gain mastery of Nos 2 and 3. But that was a personal hope. I often told him that I would never dream of entrusting him with even the smallest political mission let alone any secrets. He knew that I thought that. I never concealed my opinion.'

De Courcy's memorandum continued:

It is important to understand that Blake has a profound sense of the inevitable – of a fate which cannot be gainsaid or diverted. It was the British Minister in Korea (the late Sir Vyvyan Holt) who convinced Blake that one of the supreme inevitables was the on-surgeof Communism which could not and would not be stopped. Blake came to believe that not only was that so, but also that the future would produce a universal mind with power to plug in to individual minds and control them. If necessary that would be achieved by compulsion. He admitted that such a future repelled his emotions (Blake No 1) but that it rationalized with his intellect and attracted his desire to control and absolutely control people.

---

[1] For example, Blake never sent a word of thanks to his defence counsel Jeremy Hutchinson for his courageous pleas in mitigation of sentence nor for Hutchinson's subsequent efforts on his behalf in prison.

It is beyond comprehension why Sir Stewart Menzies, who was for so long head of MI6 and had Blake under his control, did not see all this. I saw it. Perhaps a few words about him are necessary. The natural son of the late Sir George Holford, Menzies inherited both wealth and brains.[1] His devoted mother (Mrs Menzies, later Lady Holford) used her considerable influence to have her favourite son placed on Haig's intelligence staff during World War I and from there on Menzies advanced in that particular field until he became head of the Secret Intelligence Service where he was fooled by both Philby and Blake.[2] I cannot understand how that happened, because neither Philby nor Blake were in any way suitable for such employment and on the very face of their records they were manifestly unsuitable. That could not have been clearer. It was sheer madness to employ either of them. I knew Philby's father.[3] No one brought up by him could be a safe man. Why did not Menzies realize that simple fact?

Yet Menzies was also the very man who was responsible for two such astounding successes as winning over the secret assistance of Admiral Canaris (head of the German Secret Service) and the elimination of the super dangerous Beria,[4] whose liquidation was important. I happened to be dining at White's Club with the Duke of Buccleuch on the evening of Canaris's execution. Menzies stopped at our table and said, 'I have lost my greatest friend.' I also happened to see Menzies a few days after Beria's death and he frankly told me he had played a part in that event. Yet the same man could be wholly blind to or evade matters of supreme importance. But it did not suit him to suspect Philby and Blake and he refused to do so . . .

[1] Holford, a royal equerry and a rich landowner, did not marry Mrs Menzies until 1912, although his son Stewart by her was born in 1890. Lady Holford was a daughter of Arthur Wilson of Tranby Croft, scene of the notorious baccarat scandal in 1891 in which the Prince of Wales (later King Edward VII) was involved. Holford died in 1926 and Menzies in 1968.

[2] In fairness to Menzies it should be stated that in addition to his staff job he fought in action, being mentioned in despatches and awarded the DSO and MC.

[3] St John Philby (1885–1960), explorer and orientalist. His anti-war views resulted in his internment for a short time during the Second World War, but he was eventually exonerated and freed.

[4] Beria, KGB chief under Stalin, was arrested and shot during the struggle for power which followed Stalin's death in 1953.

No one can ever say Blake lacked nerve. Defeatist he may well be, but nerve he does not lack. Nor does he lack extraordinary powers of deception. I for one have never seen Blake's capacity to deceive excelled. He possessed not one shred of truth or real loyalty in his make up – save to his mother, to whom I believe he is sincerely devoted; perhaps also to his sisters.

Finally in D Hall there was Seán Alphonsus Bourke, a thirty-year-old Irish Catholic from a respectable family of merchants in Limerick. After three years in Daingean, a notorious reformatory in Offaly (formerly King's County) for a series of petty thefts, he took the boat to England where in a short time he was sent to Borstal for receiving a wireless set knowing it to have been stolen. He was released after fifteen months and settled in Crawley, Sussex, working on a building site and then in a local factory. Although he was basically heterosexual, Bourke was also a pederast, and at this time he was arrested for interfering with boys and sentenced to a short term of imprisonment. He bore a grudge against the policeman who had arrested him and this policeman received a home-made bomb in the post. Bourke was again arrested, charged at Sussex Assizes in 1961 with sending it and pleaded not guilty. But the jury thought otherwise and this time he got seven years. In Wormwood Scrubs his behaviour was impeccable. From head cutter in the tailor's shop he progressed to being editor of the prison magazine *New Horizon* with a private office in D Hall and a 'blue band' which meant that he could go anywhere in the prison without an escort.

In addition there were two other prisoners with an Irish back-ground – Michael Reynolds and Pat Porter (these were not their real surnames). They both belonged to the Committee of 100, the nuclear disarmament group formed by Bertrand Russell, the philosopher and social reformer, who was the first President of the Campaign for Nuclear Disarmament. In 1960 he had split the CND to form the more militant Committee of 100 dedicated to civil disobedience in pursuit of its aims. Michael Reynolds and Pat Porter both helped to organize the civil disobedience demonstration at Wethersfield RAF base in December 1961, for which they were imprisoned from 1961 to 1963.

One morning in the late summer or early autumn of 1965, Blake, who had become friendly with Bourke over the years, approached him solemnly and said he had an important matter to discuss with him. 'I have a proposition to put to you,' he said, as they walked towards the end of the hall, adding that he had two preliminary points he would like to make. The first was that he possessed no capital at all, but he did represent a fairly substantial sum of money in his person, such as writing about his experiences. Secondly, if Bourke refused, Blake said he would understand perfectly and not think any the less of him. All he asked was that Bourke would think it over for a few days. Bourke replied that he understood.

'I have now been in prison for more than four years,' Blake went on. 'From the outset my sentence has always seemed to me a bit unreal, and I had hoped for some sort of relief, such as an exchange of prisoners with the Russians or something like that. However, I have now good reason to believe that such an exchange will not take place. I have therefore decided that the time has come for me to leave here . . . er . . . under my own steam, as it were. I am asking you, Seán, to help me escape.' Then, seeing that Bourke appeared surprised and too confused to answer, Blake repeated: 'You don't have to give me your answer straight away. Think it over for a few days.'

Bourke stopped and faced Blake. 'George,' he said, 'I don't have to think it over.'

'Oh?' Blake queried apprehensively. 'What have you decided?'

'I'm your man!'

Blake was enraptured by this decision. Then, Bourke said, 'Just one thing.'

'What's that?'

'Don't mention money any more.'

3

During the next few weeks Blake and Bourke spent hours discussing the details of the planned escape. They reckoned it would cost about

£700 and Blake told Bourke, who was shortly due to be released for a probationary period on parole that his mother Mrs Catherine Blake would be able to provide this sum. Blake had a snapshot of his three sons which he cut in half, giving Bourke one half and telling him that he would slip the other half to his mother during the next visit. This was to facilitate Bourke's good faith when he met Mrs Blake. During the parole period preceding Bourke's ultimate release he would get a job and was free to work at it with time off provided he slept, except at weekends, within the prison precincts in a building known as the hostel, located on the right of the main gate. Fortunately the job was in CAV Ltd, a subsidiary company of the Lucas group manufacturing car spare parts in nearby Acton. 'Bourke therefore had free access to both the prison and the outside world,' wrote de Courcy at the time. A remarkable correspondence took place between Bourke and Blake, ie between hostel and prison. No one detected it, notwithstanding that many prisoners knew about it and in fact carried the letters. In fact one unreliable courier delivered a letter intended for Blake to the wrong man, but fortunately for Blake he did not inform the prison authorities. There was also the possibility that Blake would be transferred to a top-security prison like Durham, which would completely upset the escape plan.

In due course Bourke met Blake's mother and each produced a half of the photograph, the two being placed together so that they fitted. But Mrs Blake made difficulties. First, she said that, if she were to draw £700 from her bank, the manager would be suspicious, since she only drew out small sums for shopping and the like. Bourke hinted gently that this was a hazard she might be prepared to face since her son's freedom was at stake. Mrs Blake eventually decided that this was something she could not decide alone but must ask her younger daughter Adéle, who was married to a scientist named Boswinkle and living in Baghdad. Bourke then asked Mrs Blake to let him know when Mrs Boswinkle was coming to England, and as Mrs Blake's handwriting was familiar at the prison since she often wrote to George, Bourke produced an envelope which he stamped and on which he wrote his name and address, telling her to use it when she wrote to him and to sign the letter 'Jean'.

Mrs Blake was nervous. 'I'm frightened of all this,' she said. 'If anything goes wrong, I hate to think of poor George being sent to that dreadful Durham prison with all those train robbers. At least now he is fairly comfortable and I can write to him regularly.'

'But, Mrs Blake,' said Bourke, 'he is bound to be sent to a top-security prison sooner or later anyway. It's amazing he hasn't been transferred already, especially since those two train robbers escaped.[1] After all he is serving twelve years longer than any of the train robbers, and his escape would be much more embarrassing for the British Government than anyone else's. Indeed this operation of ours is a race against time.'

Several weeks later Bourke heard from Mrs Catherine Blake, a brief note in the envelope on which Bourke had written his name and address, telling him that Adéle would be coming to England some months later, in February 1966. The three duly met for dinner in the Cumberland Hotel near Marble Arch. Mother and daughter insisted that Bourke should be their guest. In spite of their hospitality – Adéle paid for the meal with wine and other drinks – it was an unsatisfactory meeting, at least for Bourke. Adéle wanted to know the details, which Bourke gave her reluctantly, explaining how Blake proposed to escape from the cinema and how Bourke would be waiting for him with a rope ladder. 'Naturally George and I know Wormwood Scrubs like the backs of our hands,' said Bourke, 'and we both feel we have a very good chance.'

'And what happens after he escapes – if he does escape?' Adéle queried.

Bourke told her with considerable patience, though he had difficulty in controlling his temper, that George would hide out for a while and then leave the country on a false passport.

'And where will you get the passport?'

Bourke dismissed this foolish question with the contempt it

---

[1] The Great Train Robbery took place on 8 August 1963 on the Glasgow–London express near Aylesbury. Twelve of the robbers were sentenced to thirty years each, having got away with £2½ millions, of which only £500,000 was recovered. Charles Wilson, a bookmaker, escaped in 1964, and Ronald Biggs, a carpenter, in 1965. Biggs reached Brazil, where he married a Brazilian woman, on which ground his extradition was refused by the Brazilian Government.

deserved. 'I haven't spent five years in prison for nothing. I know where to get a passport all right. That is a mere formality.'

However, Adéle remained unconvinced. 'I really do not have very much faith in your plans,' she said. 'It all seems too easy to be true. Throwing a rope ladder over a prison wall, just like that!'

'Mrs Boswinkle,' replied Bourke, his patience almost at breaking point. 'The execution of the escape is my responsibility and obviously I am more qualified to judge the merit of my plans. Plans, incidentally, which your brother helped me draw up.'

'That may be so,' she said. 'But it is my mother and I who are being asked to finance the project, and I would have to be satisfied that you were going to succeed before I would agree to help.'

'I cannot give you a hundred per cent guarantee that I am going to succeed. Nobody can ever do that before the event, except, of course, in fiction. This is real life. We won't know if we are going to succeed until we try – and I would like to try.'

Adéle now asked to inspect George's post-escape accommodation and made other unrealistic demands, such as how was Bourke going to get her brother out of the country. She also wanted to see a detailed list of expenses. 'I don't see how you could possibly need so much money,' she concluded.

'You cannot inspect the accommodation and the passport until they have been arranged, and they cannot be arranged until I get the money. And I can assure you that £700 is the very minimum that would be required. This figure, in fact, was suggested by your brother.'

Adéle was still not satisfied, nor was her mother who had deliberately left the talking to her. They told Bourke that they were going to see George in a few days and would talk the matter over with him. All Bourke could do was to say he hoped the matter would be settled without further delay. 'March is nearly upon us,' he added, 'and our present plans are geared to carrying out the escape under cover of darkness. Even if the money is forthcoming it is going to take another month to make the final preparations. There is no time to lose.'

'I met the two ladies yesterday and was very concerned at their nervous state,' George Blake wrote to Bourke in a note smuggled into the hostel. 'They are obviously very worried about all this and I have reluctantly come to the conclusion that they should no longer be involved, for their own sakes as well as ours. I appreciate that this will be a great disappointment to you, especially as you have tried so hard. Can you think of any other way in which the funds might be raised?'

Apart from the financial problem this was an unsatisfactory means of communication and would be more so when Bourke was released and Blake's notes would have to go to some outside place such as a pub where Bourke could pick them up. Thus Blake might miss the news of some sudden change of routine which might upset his plans. For instance, there were two escapes towards the end of March, which were by way of the east wall behind D Hall facing Artillery Road and Hammersmith Hospital, the favourite mode of escape as the authorities knew. They now stationed a prison officer permanently at the corner where the north and east walls met, commanding a clear view of both. This was all right when the weather was fine, but when it rained the officer had to take shelter in the kiosk at the end of D Hall. When he did this, he could still keep an eye on the north wall, but not on the east wall facing Hammersmith Hospital.

Bourke continued for some time to be worried by the problem of communication. Suddenly he had a brainwave. Why shouldn't he communicate with Blake direct in his cell with a small 'walkie-talkie' or two-way radio which would fit in his pocket? With this end in view he wrote to the prison officer in charge of the hostel, asking for £25 from his accumulated savings 'for the purpose of buying a new suit'. His request was granted and next day he went to Piccadilly and looked into the front window of the McDonald Stores, which dealt in radio and other electrical equipment. There he saw what he wanted, a pair of Japanese two-way radios in black leather cases small enough to fit into a man's inside pocket. The price ticket showed that they cost £35 but as there was a sale the price had been marked down to £25; it also indicated that the range was five miles.

Bourke went into the shop and bought the walkie-talkies. The salesman explained to him – what he already knew – that the range was from one hill top to another or across an open space and the sea, but would be much shorter if there were intervening objects.

[68]

However, this suited Bourke as he was sure that half or even a quarter of a mile would be sufficient for his purpose. Asked by the salesman where he would be using them, Bourke replied that it would be in a large farm in the country where communications were apt to be difficult. First the walkie-talkies were tested, Bourke staying in the shop while the salesman went out into the street. They worked perfectly and the salesman obligingly included a spare set of batteries in the parcel, adding that if Bourke had any trouble with them to bring them back and he could try something else. In due course Bourke walked through the prison gate to the hostel with his parcel. 'Been shopping, Seán?' said the gatekeeper. 'Yes,' said Bourke, 'all the way to Piccadilly.' He knew he would not be asked to open the parcel, since a hostel inmate in those days could bring in a suitcase without any search.

The next thing Bourke had to do was to work out call-signs and an identifying code for use in transmission. For the call-signs Bourke decided to use two of the best-known figures in Irish patriotic mythology – Finn MacCumhail and his henchman Baldy Canaan – who flourished in the second century AD and were forerunners of the modern Fenian Brotherhood. Thus, in the phonetic alphabet Bourke would be 'Fox Michael' and Blake 'Baker Charlie'. As for the identifying code, Bourke chose an appropriate quotation from the seventeenth-century royalist poet Richard Lovelace. Thus the code would run:

Bourke: Stone walls do not a prison make, nor iron bars a cage.
Blake: Minds innocent and quiet take this for a hermitage.
Bourke: Richard Lovelace must have been a fool.
Blake: Or just a dreamer.

4

Bourke wrote the call-signs and code signals in a letter to Blake which he entrusted to a young courier who unfortunately delivered it to the wrong man whom he mistook for Blake. The recipient promptly passed it on to Blake without telling the authorities. Bourke then enlisted the help of another prisoner called Peter, to whom he gave Blake's walkie-talkie during a theatre show in the dark, at the same time letting him into the secret that he was going to 'spring' Blake. Since Peter could not pass on the walkie-talkie until next day, they agreed to test it out that night between them, Peter in his cell and Bourke in the hostel. It worked perfectly, as it did the following night when Bourke called Blake at the pre-arranged time of 10.30 pm when Bourke could see that lights were out in the top gallery of D Hall.

Bourke duly pressed the transmitting button. 'This is Fox Michael calling Baker Charlie, Fox Michael calling Baker Charlie. Come in, please. Over.' Bourke released the button and listened. There was a short pause, and then, to his satisfaction, he heard the hum induced by the pressing of the other set's transmitting button. The answering voice was unmistakably Blake's with its pronounced Dutch accent. 'This is Baker Charlie to Fox Michael, Baker Charlie to Fox Michael. Receiving you loud and clear. Over.' Lovelace's verses and the other call-signs followed.

As might be expected Blake was thrilled and excited. 'This is my first really free and unrestricted contact with the outside world for five years,' he began. 'It really is a wonderful feeling!' So wonderful, in fact, that they talked for the best part of two hours, finally agreeing that further talks must be shorter in order to save the batteries. In the course of their prolonged conversation, Blake said he was lying comfortably on his bed with the aerial fully extended, but he had shut the window as a precaution against being heard by any passing night patrol on the gallery outside. Also he had his ordinary radio tuned in to a musical programme in case he might be heard by any neighbouring inmates or by hidden listening devices. After agreeing that financial help from 'the two ladies' was out, Bourke said he thought he might be able to get help from Michael Reynolds, with whom he had been friends in Wormwood Scrubs since their mothers were both Irish Catholics. Bourke would be seeing him at the weekend and would call Blake back at the same time on Monday.

'If this man does agree to help with money, it will not be possible to carry out the operation before your release, will it?' Blake queried.

'No, I'm afraid not,' answered Bourke. 'It is now the middle of May. I shall be moving from here in about six weeks, hardly enough time to do all that has to be done . . . In the meantime I will keep you informed of progress. And, of course, you yourself will be busy trying to work out a way of getting out of D Hall.'

Michael Reynolds lived with his wife Anne in a modest house in Camden Town bought on mortgage. He was a socialist but not a Communist and as we have seen he belonged to the Committee of 100 which had hived off from the Campaign for Nuclear Disarmament (CND). He was sympathetic when Bourke told him of his problem. 'I think I will be able to raise the £700 all right,' he said. 'It will take a little time, but I'll start to work on it next week.' The only other thing Michael wished to know was what was the penalty for helping someone to escape from prison.

'The maximum is five years' imprisonment,' said Bourke. 'And out of five years you serve three years and four months for good behaviour.'

'Very well, Seán,' said Michael. 'We're with you!' Anne agreed and they shook hands.

Bourke relayed this news to Blake as arranged, and Blake outlined his plan to get out at the south end of D Hall, opposite the end where the screw was stationed. If Bourke threw a rope ladder over, when Blake dropped to the ground he would only be fifteen yards from the perimeter wall with the rope ladder facing Hammersmith Hospital, whereas the screw would be a hundred yards away at the north end and so unable to catch the escaper if he lost no time in climbing the wall.

Bourke and Blake continued to converse by walkie-talkie. Then, one day a young fellow inmate named Roy Fletcher picked up the conversation on his own radio. Fletcher had been jailed for life for being accessory to murder, burning down a house in which several people died. As a 'lifer' he enjoyed a number of privileges including a radio. Next morning he saw Blake in his cell and said: 'What about Fox Michael?' Blake went deadly pale and tried to laugh it off. But he realized that now another was in the secret. However, luck was with him, since Fletcher decided to remain silent and did so. Fletcher always denied that he was responsible for burning down the house in his case and he was desperately anxious to have his case reopened and consequently not to become involved in any incident that might adversely affect this possibility. Also no doubt he was aware that Blake had some very violent friends among the other prisoners. In Kenneth de Courcy's words, 'It would certainly have cost the man who spoke a very heavy price if he had, because Blake had lined up some of the toughest and most popular men who would certainly have beaten to pulp anyone suspected of talking.'

Furthermore, Fletcher, who told de Courcy that he had listened to between thirty and forty walkie-talkie transmissions between Blake and Bourke, admitted to de Courcy that 'if words have any meaning at all' Bourke did not know that Blake planned eventually to go to Russia.

The entire gist of the talks was that Blake had no hope from anyone at all – save Bourke himself – and that once over the wall he would be in Bourke's hands. In his replies Bourke never once mentioned flight to Russia but only refuge in Ireland . . .

Two letters from Bourke to Blake which a prisoner showed me, and which dealt with the planned escape, contained not one hint of flight to Russia. In his talks with me Blake stressed that whatever happened he would never go to Russia. In a talk with a prisoner just before the escape Blake said that the Russians would be even more surprised than the English. So he really did lay it on. Indeed I have heard this so often repeated by prisoners that I myself believe it must be true.

Bourke was released on 4 June 1966, and he took a 'bed-sitter' in Perryn Road about ten minutes' drive from the prison. During the following nights he repeated the call-sign into the walkie-talkie but without success, keeping it up for half an hour each time and then abandoning it. Of course, what had happened was that Blake was out of range. Although only a mile from the prison, communications were prevented by the numerous buildings in such a built-up area. This is how de Courcy described it from Blake's side:

Night after night Blake tried to make contact. All was silent. Blake, himself the great betrayer, began to think he had been himself sold out. On one terrible night when lying in his cell desperately trying to get into contact by walkie-talkie the night watchman switched on Blake's cell light. That – thought Blake – was it. But it was not. The watchman noticed nothing amiss.

Blake now began to pump people about Bourke's character. Could an Irishman be relied on? Why should he risk so much? Had the sweets of liberty so greatly attracted Bourke that the thought of another conviction scared him off? All these anguished doubts and fears coursed through Blake's mind. He ate little, talked less. People began to ask what was wrong. Most put it down to his coming divorce – but some knew what the real cause was.[1]

Suddenly Blake made contact again . . .

What happened was that Bourke went along Old Oak Common Lane and entered the park north of the prison, lying down in the grass near the north wall, calling to Blake on the walke-talkie as he went along. 'Nothing to report,' said Bourke. 'I tried on Monday from my new address and I assume you were also trying.'

'Yes,' said Blake. 'I was trying too, as agreed. We were out of range. I have one piece of information for you. About that kiosk in the corner, a phone has now been installed and the authorities are confident that the whole place can be surrounded within four minutes of the alarm being raised. How does this affect you?'

'It leaves me quite unperturbed,' Bourke told the prisoner. 'All *we* need is two minutes at the very most. If four minutes is the best they can do, then they have already lost the contest. Actually I am even relieved that they are so confident; they will become complacent about further measures. As you know, there is nothing much I can do at the moment: I am waiting for funds. I shall be seeing my friend again in a few days. Can we talk again next Saturday night at the same time?'

[1] On 18 June 1966 it was announced that Blake had filed a petition for divorce, apparently wishing to free his wife to marry again, although she had stood by him for several years after his conviction.

'Yes,' said Blake, 'and I think we had better sign off now.'

'Right,' Bourke concluded. 'This is Fox Michael to Baker Charlie. Over and out. Good night.'

Bourke folded his aerial, put the walkie-talkie into his pocket and walked to the centre of the park, so as to put as much distance between himself and the prison before turning into Braybrook Street north-west of Wormwood Scrubs. As it was, a police patrol car approached as he turned into the street. The car slowed down, its occupants eyed him for a few moments and then to Bourke's relief, passed on its way. It would have been awkward if the police had recognized Bourke, stopped and searched him, and found the walkie-talkie in his pocket.

5

It was a near miracle that Blake was not transferred to a maximum security prison at this time, which would have ruined his escape plans. The Governor of Wormwood Scrubs, Mr Thomas Hayes, recommended it more than once, but the Home Office through the Prison Commissioners absolutely refused to move him. In fact, on the contrary, they took him out of such security as he was in and made him manager of the canteen which gave him complete liberty to move about the prison a good deal. Thus they did the exact opposite of what the Governor advised. The Governor's original recommendation was due to the discovery of an earlier escape plan of Blake's, which Blake had concerted with an American airline pilot named Andrew Newton, the idea being that Newton, who was imprisoned for illicitly possessing and using a firearm should go too.[1] However, Newton appears to have quarrelled with Blake and wrote a letter with the details to MI6 – to the organization and not

---

[1] Newton was again sentenced to imprisonment in 1976, when he attempted to kill the Liberal leader Jeremy Thorpe's friend Norman Scott at the same time killing Scott's dog. On this occasion he got two years. See H. Montgomery Hyde's *A Tangled Web* (1986) p 235.

to any particular individual – and asked de Courcy who was allowed to visit his solicitor at his office in the City to post it for him. De Courcy refused but told his solicitor who advised him to see the Governor and tell him what he knew. This de Courcy did with some reluctance and was told by the Governor that he had done the right thing.

'As to Bourke,' de Courcy wrote in his memorandum in Wormwood Scrubs, 'he is a natural good friend in need and Blake was more than lucky to meet him; he was a far better friend than Blake is ever likely to prove. That is not to say that I in any way dislike Blake. But I regard him as a man devoid of mercy. Bourke is a very different character altogether and I am rather worried about his eventual fate.'

A high official told me that the authorities were pretty well satisfied that Blake plans to liquidate everyone who really knows anything important. He would liquidate Seán Bourke without compunction if he thought it necessary. For that I should be sorry, because the truth is that Seán Bourke possesses the very qualities of enterprise, skill and *élan* which are badly needed. Moreover he is the very soul of loyalty to any cause he espouses so long as it remains loyal to its purpose. I do not think Seán Bourke should be written off as a bad man. He is a man of exaggerated reactions, which is another matter.

I am positive that if Blake had allowed it to be known that he was still a Communist and was planning to go to Russia, he would not have received the help he did. But he lied to all concerned and he successfully persuaded others that he would never again help Russia. Indeed he went still further and gave assurances that his object was to pay the debt which he owed to England. All that was false and a lie.

During the summer months while Blake and Bourke continued to keep in contact by walkie-talkie, prison security was strengthened. First, there was a mass break-out of six prisoners, who used the same route which Blake and Bourke had planned to use. Four of the escapers had been involved in a bad case of rape, their trial judge telling them that they were worse than animals. The other two were serving equally long sentences for causing grievous bodily harm. The escape took place in the morning between 7 and 8 am when the telephone kiosk was regularly left unmanned for an hour. The Home Secretary, Roy Jenkins, visited the prison and appeared on television the same evening, assuring the public there was no need for worry since the escape was due to a loophole in the security system which had now been plugged. But he did not say what the loophole was. He indicated that one of the new security measures would be the installation of closed-circuit television in the prison.

Further security measures followed the shooting of three policemen in Braybrook Street. In the intensive and prolonged investigation which followed the murders, it was eventually established that the killings were not connected with any of the prison inmates, since none of them was missing at the time. There was a rumour that the prison was to be monitored for illicit radio communications, but if this was done those between Blake and Bourke were undetected.

Meanwhile, some money came in from CND sources and this enabled Bourke to buy a second-hand Humber Hawk with a good engine and brakes for £60. It was a 1955 model, the registration number being 117 GMX. Bourke unplugged the aerial lead from the car radio and clamped it to the cap of the folded-down aerial of the walkie-talkie. Thus he could and did communicate through the car's own aerial, and he hid the walkie-talkie in a pot of chrysanthemums, smelling them for the benefit of any passer-by who might look through the windscreen or doors. 'What could be more natural,' wrote Bourke afterwards, 'than a man sitting in his car holding a bunch of flowers outside Hammersmith Hospital as he waited for the visiting hour to begin?'

In his next conversation with Blake, Bourke suggested that, assuming the escape succeeded, they might leave the country on the same night. One possible route was to travel to Ireland immediately, either in disguise or hidden in a vehicle on the car ferry, and catch a plane to the Continent next morning from Shannon Airport, after driving south through Ireland during the night. Bourke had studied all the relevant timetables and he felt it was just possible. But Blake rejected this ploy, considering it better to go into hiding immediately and plan the final exit at leisure. 'OK,' Bourke agreed. 'Actually this makes things easier!'

Bourke's next chore was the construction of a suitable rope-ladder to throw over the prison wall. At Woolworth's in Old Oak Common Lane he found they were selling clothes-lines thirty-six foot long. He bought three, two to serve as uprights and the third to be cut up for the rungs. Ordinary rope ladders have wooden rungs, but these would be too heavy to throw over an eighteen-foot high wall, not to mention the noise caused by the rungs striking the brick. Two doors away there was a shop selling fabrics, women's under-wear, wool and nylon thread and knitting-needles. At the knitting-needle counter Bourke chose a No 13. These needles were made of steel, covered in grey plastic, and measured fourteen inches in length, to reinforce the nylon thread, which would give a generous margin on either side of the twelve-inch-wide ladder.

'I'll have thirty,' Bourke told the woman in charge of the counter.

'Your wife must be doing a lot of knitting,' she said, raising her eyebrows and smiling.

'They're not really for knitting,' Bourke told her. 'They're for my pupils at school. It's amazing the abstracts these young art students can produce from simple things like knitting needles.'

The next three evenings after work Bourke carefully constructed the ladder, using the knitting needles to reinforce the nylon thread and stiffen the rungs. When there was a knock on the door from the landlord coming to empty the gas meter or something similar, Bourke threw the unfinished ladder under the bed before answering the door.

When the job was finished, Bourke set out to calculate the time it would take the police at Shepherd's Bush station to reach the prison after they had been alerted. Incidentally the three police officers murdered in Braybrook Street had belonged to this station. Two of the killers had been caught and there was a big manhunt on for the third. Driving from the station via Uxbridge Road, Wood Lane, the BBC television studios and the White City Stadium, to Du Cane Road, he pulled up opposite Artillery Road. The journey took five minutes. He repeated it several times but could not make it under five minutes even when the various traffic lights were with him. Hence Bourke reckoned he would have a comfortable margin, since within three minutes of throwing the ladder over the prison wall he and Blake could be out of Du Cane Road, while the police when alerted would take at least six minutes plus the time spent in assembling them. Even if the police were to set out at the same moment as the escape, which would be impossible, Bourke was certain they could still make it. There was, too, a slight additional advantage in that Latimer Road marks the boundary between the metropolitan boroughs of Hammersmith and Kensington, and High-lever Road where he was eventually to find accommodation was just in Kensington so that the initial police activity of the Shepherd's Bush station would be confined to the area west of Latimer Road.

After consulting his friend Michael Reynolds, Bourke fixed the escape date for Saturday 22 October 1966. The next thing was to find a flat as the bed-sitter in Perryn Street was too small for two and in any event the landlady would no doubt not agree. Paradoxically the more Bourke was prepared to pay in rent, the more difficult it was to secure the necessary accommodation. He went to several of the better-class agencies, staffed with pretty girls wearing mini-skirts and speaking with debs' accents. 'Oh, yes, madam, he's British all right,' one would phone a prospective landlord or landlady. 'Oh, of course, *white* . . . Well, he's a journalist . . . Perhaps you wouldn't mind interviewing him yourself. Good! I'll send him along.'

Everywhere the story was the same. Journalists, especially of the freelance variety, were regarded with disfavour. Also references were demanded. It was in vain for Bourke to say that he had just returned to Britain after ten years in Australia and offer to pay a month's rent in advance – in cash. One had to have references.

Bourke now decided to go to Ireland for a week and see his mother, whom he had not seen for five years. He would try again for a flat when he got back and told Blake he would contact him on Tuesday 18 October, four days before the escape date. Accordingly he bought a single ticket from Aer Lingus in his own name, saw his mother and some old friends in Limerick, and at the end of the week bought a single ticket from Shannon to Heathrow in the name of Sullivan. 'I'm off to Dublin now,' he told his mother when they said good-bye. He added that he intended to spend the next few months writing in a house lent to him by a friend and would not be going back to England 'till next year sometime'. As they parted, Mrs Bourke gave her son a religious medal and splashed him with holy water since she was extremely devout. An hour later Seán was in Shannon drinking a lot of whiskey to cheer himself up and two hours after that he was back in London.

On the Monday he went to a working-class agency in Paddington. There were no debs in mini-skirts, but Bourke got what he wanted – a flatlet at 28 Highlever Road, North Kensington, the rent being £4 15s a week. He filled in the form he was handed, giving his name as M. Sigsworth and his address as 5 Bank Road, Croydon, which in fact did not exist. Highlever Road was ideal, since the flatlet was about three minutes' drive from Wormwood Scrubs. Going east from the prison along Du Cane Road, one came to traffic lights at the junction with Wood Lane, but when the lights were red there was filtering for drivers turning left while those turning right had to wait for the lights to change to green. Opposite Hammersmith school there was North Pole Road, which led either direct or via Latimer Road and Oxford Gardens to Highlever Road, the latter route being rather shorter since No 28 was at the Oxford Gardens end.

Bourke was accepted without question at 28 Highlever Road, paying a month's rent in advance plus the agency fee. He was given three keys, one to the front door and the others to the two rooms, a bed-sitting room and a kitchen-cum-bathroom. This was the only flatlet in the house with its own kitchen and bathroom, the other rooms being separate bedsitters whose occupants used a communal bathroom. It suited perfectly since there was no danger of Blake being disturbed after he had reached the flatlet.

On Tuesday evening, 18 October, Bourke called Blake as arranged and went over the details of the escape plan for the 22nd. Bourke would park his car in Artillery Road opposite the end of D Hall and call Blake at six o'clock precisely. Assuming that the coast was clear he would signal him to go to the window and break the iron frame for which he had had the necessary implement smuggled in. This was a car-jack. Blake was to call back when this had been done and Bourke would then tell him to climb out of the window and drop down. Finally Blake would call him again from the ground beside the prison wall when Bourke would indicate that the ladder was coming over the wall. 'The moment you see the ladder you will run to it and climb up,' said Bourke. 'You must not delay as we must assume that the man on guard will see the ladder at the same moment. We must both keep our radios on throughout and each of us must be prepared to give the other immediate warning if anything goes wrong.'

Again, assuming all went well, Blake was to get into the back seat of the car where he would find a mackintosh and a hat. In the right-hand pocket of the mac he would find an envelope with some money for telephone calls together with a slip of paper giving a coded telephone number if they were separated, so that Blake could communicate with Bourke's friends, who would take over should Bourke be caught. He did not give either the code for the telephone number or the address in Highlever Road, which he would do when Blake was safely in the car. In the left-hand pocket of the mac were the keys of the front door and the rooms in the flatlet, since the idea was that Bourke would stop the car round the corner from the house and Blake would make his way in alone. In the bed-sitting room Blake would find a suit of civilian clothes to change into, as well as a television set and a transistor radio. 'The radio will be tuned into the BBC Home Service, so you only have to switch it on to hear the news. You will also get a news bulletin on television about nine o'clock when you should be able to hear about the escape.' Meanwhile Bourke would drive the car as far away as possible. If he should be caught in the process and Blake should hear an announcement that 'a man is helping the police with their inquiries', he should not believe it. 'I shall definitely *not* be helping the bastards!' Bourke added emphatically.

Following the earlier break-out, wire grids had been placed across the windows in the galleries of A, B and C Halls but not yet in D Hall. 'Today being Tuesday,' said Blake, 'there is a strong possibility we will not have them in D Hall by Saturday.' 'My God,' Bourke replied, 'I can hardly believe it! Somebody in there likes us.' 'Yes,'

Blake laughed. 'That grid would be quite a nuisance.' Indeed it would, since cutting through quarter inch wires would cause a lot of noise. 'Let's keep our fingers crossed that nothing will change before Saturday,' Blake concluded.

6

So far luck was with them, since when Bourke called at noon the escape window had not been fitted with a grid. 'Everything is ready here for this evening,' Blake went on. 'The conditions are perfect. Most of the others will be at the cinema, and there will be only two officers in the hall.'

Bourke spent the rest of the fateful day before the final take-off, doing various chores, shopping, buying another pot of chrysanthemums, and testing the rope-ladder again for strength and practising throwing it. By 4.45 a light drizzle was falling, which developed into heavy rain during the next hour, which Bourke welcomed, since rain would not encourage people to loiter in the street, affecting visibility along the inadequately lit prison walls and obscuring the view from the look-out kiosk with its telephone in D Gallery. At 5.15 Bourke drove down East Acton Lane to The Vale, Uxbridge, turning on the radio and buying some chocolate sweets to steady his nerves. A cigarette would have done for this purpose but he was a non-smoker. He sat in the car for a while near the King's Arms pub where a pretty young barmaid used to serve him a pint of Guinness at lunch time when he worked nearby. For Seán Bourke liked pretty girls although in fact he was bisexual.

At 5.45 he returned along East Acton Lane to Old Oak Road. At the Western Circus roundabout junction on the A40, between Western Avenue and Westway, there was a traffic jam controlled by a policeman who after a wait turned round facing Old Oak Lane and waved Bourke on. Accordingly he proceeded along Old Oak Common Lane to the entrance to Du Cane Road where there was a gap in the queue. Driving slowly past the prison gate he turned left into Artillery Road, going to the top and doing a three-point turn, and then stopping at the agreed point between the prison wall and the side entrance to Hammersmith Hospital. It was now just after five past six. 'Sorry for the delay,' Bourke now called into the transmitter. 'But everything is OK out here just now. Are you ready to proceed?' Blake replied that he was and his friend who had undertaken to break the window bars was standing beside him with the jack in his hand. 'Tell him to proceed *now*,' said Bourke. Three minutes later Blake called back to say that the window had been 'taken care of' and Blake was ready to make his exit.

Bourke was about to press the transmitter-button again when a pair of strongly shining headlights lit up Artillery Road. The vehicle to which they belonged passed Bourke's car slowly and in the screen mirror Bourke could see that they belonged to a van. He deliberately smelled the chrysanthemums and the van went to the top of Artillery Road where it disappeared into the park.

'Are you still there?' Bourke called.

'Yes,' was the reply. 'What happened?'

'A van has just gone into the park,' said Bourke. 'I think it's a groundsman or patrolman or something like that, gone to check on the sports pavilion. He will be coming back, of course, so I cannot let you climb out of the window yet. As soon as he is gone, I will give you the signal to proceed.'

Five minutes later the headlights reappeared at the top of Artillery Road. The driver got out to padlock the barrier into the park as Bourke correctly surmised. He then got into the van and crept past the Humber Hawk with Bourke still smelling the flowers. Bourke now realized that not only was he being scrutinized but was also under suspicion. The van driver again got out of his vehicle with an Alsatian dog on a short lead. Bourke hoped that the van driver would realize that he was waiting for the hospital opening hour, but the driver stood his ground and from his appearance it was obvious that he was a security guard. If a policeman had been handy, he would have called him. In view of this confrontation there was nothing that Bourke could do but leave.

Accordingly he drove down Artillery Road into Du Cane Road, turned left and then went on to Wood Lane where he turned right and along Wood Lane into Westway, then right again into Du Cane Road. When he reached Artillery Road, the van had gone but there was a car where the van had first passed him and which turned out to contain a courting couple. Bourke had to get rid of them and by staring hard he made them feel embarrassed and they eventually made off. Responding to Bourke's call, Blake said: 'I cannot delay here any longer. They're on their way back from the cinema. I must come out now.' 'OK Baker Charlie,' answered Bourke. 'Go ahead.' A minute or two later Blake announced that he was out. 'You can throw the ladder now,' he said. But another car now drove into Artillery Road, probably visitors to the hospital. 'Hang on just a minute,' Bourke called. 'There are some people here. I must wait for them to go.' 'Very well,' answered Blake. 'But I hope they'll go soon. I am already out of the hall and waiting here for the ladder. The men are back from the cinema. The patrol might come along any minute. Please hurry.'

It was now 6.45 pm. The car's occupants got out, the lights being switched off, and they walked towards Du Cane Road, clearly on their way to the hospital. Still another car appeared and parked by the first one with its headlights on. 'Fox Michael! Fox Michael! Come in please!' shouted Blake. 'I can't wait much longer.' Bourke got out of the Humber and walked towards the other vehicle in which there was a man and a woman. They also made for the hospital. Meanwhile Blake was panicking, since it was five minutes to seven. 'Fox Michael! You must throw the ladder now, *you simply must*. There is no more time!' Meanwhile yet another car had appeared with its lights shining. Disregarding this vehicle as he could not see who was in it, Bourke got out, took the rope ladder from the boot, climbed on to the roof of the Humber and threw the ladder over the prison wall. He then jumped down and pulled his end of the ladder a couple of yards to the right as otherwise Blake might have landed on the car roof and gone through it. Bourke also left the pot of chrysanthemums by the wall since he would have no further use for them.

Eventually Blake appeared at the top of the wall, and straddling the coping for a few seconds looked down, lowered himself on the outside, hanging on by his hands. 'Jump!' shouted Bourke, at which

Blake let go throwing himself outwards. Bourke tried but failed to break his fall and in a moment Blake was sprawling at Bourke's feet, his head having hit the gravelled road. He lay still and groaned. 'George,' said Bourke as he bent down. 'Are you all right? For Christ's sake what's the matter with you?' Fortunately they were both shielded by Bourke's car, while Bourke dragged Blake towards the rear door which he had left open, and pushed Blake, still groaning, on to the back seat. He then got in himself behind the driving wheel. As he did so the headlights of the other car were switched off, and its occupants, a man, a woman and a girl, got out, the two females chatting in the middle of the road while the man locked the car. Bourke started up the engine and grinding into second gear moved off to the astonishment of the two women who jumped out of the way. There was a gap in the traffic and Bourke was able to turn into Du Cane Road without delay.

It was now raining heavily and the windscreen was steamed up, since Bourke had had to keep the windows closed when exchanging calls with Blake on the walkie-talkie. Bourke now began to wipe the windscreen with his hand when he saw a car in front of him. The car stopped suddenly at a zebra crossing opposite the hospital's main entrance. Bourke slammed on his brakes and his front bumper hit the other car's rear bumper with a resounding crash. People had finished crossing, but the car ahead waited a minute or two before moving, its driver pulling into the kerb and signalling Bourke to pull in ahead of him.

'Some bloody hope,' muttered Bourke as he pressed the accelerator hard, changing noisily from second to third gear and screeching away towards Wood Lane. The lights were red but changed to green as he filtered left and turned into North Pole Road where the lights were also green. There were no more lights, and when he reached Latimer Road he looked back and saw they were not being followed. Meanwhile Blake had recovered somewhat. 'The phone number is written on a small piece of paper in the envelope in the right-hand pocket of the mac,' Bourke said. 'The code is simple. You just subtract *one* from each figure. Thus five means four and eight means seven. The first three figures correspond to the exchange letters. Have you got that?'

'Yes, that's perfectly clear,' said Blake.

'The address is 28 Highlever Road,' Bourke went on. 'I'm taking you there anyway.'

They stopped near the house and when they got out Bourke saw that Blake's face was streaming with blood. Nor could Blake hand over the key, since his left hand was limp and he could not put it into the pocket.

'Look's as if you've sprained it,' said Bourke.

'I'm afraid it's broken,' said Blake, and this was clear when he held up his hand. Then he added emotionally: 'Seán, you are a great fellow!' But Bourke brushed this aside. 'We'll discuss all that later,' he said. 'First things first.'

Bourke took Blake into the flatlet. 'Well, here we are,' he said. 'It isn't much but it's the best we could do. And anyway it's only temporary. There are your clothes on the bed. I hope you'll be able to change into them. There's a wash basin in the corner so you can wash your face without having to go into the bathroom.'

Bourke then lit the gas fire, took the front-door key off his key ring and handed the other two keys on the ring to Blake. 'I'll get rid of the car now,' he told Blake, adding that he would be gone about an hour. 'Lock this door after me,' he added. 'When I come back I'll knock three times.' As he left, he apologized for there not being any drink. 'It's the one thing I forgot!' However, he promised to bring some back with him.

Before leaving the house Bourke telephoned Michael Reynolds to tell him, much to his delight, that the 'operation' had been 'successfully completed'. He then drove to the bottom of Oxford Gardens, turning right into Ladbroke Grove and so on to Notting Hill Gate and Bayswater Road. He cruised about feeling elated and turned off somewhere, finally fetching up at a point which he thought was far enough away from Highlever Road. But in his elation he had been to some extent moving in a circle. In the thoroughfare where he stopped he saw from the street sign that it was Harvist Road NW6 between Harrow Road and Kilburn, near Queen's Park underground station. There he got out, went into a pub, downed four large whiskies, bought a bottle of whisky and a bottle of brandy. Then, leaving the car in Harvist Road, he caught a taxi and paid off the driver round the corner from Highlever Road. Letting himself in, he knocked three times on the door of the flatlet, which Blake opened cautiously. He had changed into the clothes Bourke had left and looked quite smart. But the blood kept oozing out of the cuts on his forehead. However, when Bourke examined it he pronounced them superficial. 'About your wrist,' he added, 'there is nothing we can do about it tonight, but tomorrow.' Meanwhile Bourke made a sling from Blake's prison shirt for his wrist.

Offered a drink Blake opted for brandy, while Bourke took a large tot of whisky which he called 'the hard stuff', as they do in Ireland.

It was now close on nine o'clock and Bourke turned on the television. The current programme was just ending and then the screen went blank. A few moments later a photograph of Blake filled the whole screen. 'High drama in West London tonight!' the announcer began. He continued:

George Blake, the double agent who was serving forty-two years' imprisonment for spying for the Russians, escaped from Wormwood Scrubs Prison in London this evening . . . A Home Office statement said that Blake was missed from his cell at seven o'clock roll call, when all the prisoners were being locked away for the night. A search was made of the prison grounds but no trace of Blake could be found . . . A huge manhunt has been launched under the direction of Scotland Yard's Special Branch. Careful watch is being kept at all airports and harbours, and East European embassies are also being kept under observation. News is still coming in of this dramatic escape and we will keep you informed.

Bourke raised his glass and, quoting Mark Antony in Shakespeare's *Julius Caesar*, said: 'Mischief, thou art afoot, take thou what course thou wilt!' Both men drank to this prophetic toast. Bourke had learned the quotation during his English literature classes in Wormwood Scrubs.

Next morning Bourke went out and bought all the newspapers he could find. They were all full of the news of the escape and stated that the Prime Minister Harold Wilson had been informed at Chequers. After they had digested the contents of the papers, Bourke went off to find a doctor. 'We must get a doctor,' he told Michael Reynolds, 'we just *must*. If we don't, I'll have to take George to a hospital tonight and say that he's a brother of mine who has just fallen down the stairs, or something.'

'That would be dangerous, wouldn't it? I mean with his photograph on every front page.' Then, after pausing for a few moments' thought, Michael said he thought he could get a doctor. 'There is a doctor I know of who might be sympathetic. He is not a friend of mine personally, but a friend of a friend.'

Michael then left the room and several minutes later came back to say that he had arranged to see his friend later that day and he would take him to the doctor. 'We must just now hope that the doctor will be available and prepared to help.' He added that if the doctor was not at home they would have to chase round a bit.

This was indeed the case. The first doctor was out of town and the second was also away and it was 7.0 pm before he was tracked down. Michael then phoned Bourke at Highlever Road to say that he could expect a visit within an hour or so.

At 8.30 the front door bell rang three times and Bourke walked to the door which he opened. Michael Reynolds was standing there with a man of about forty-five carrying a doctor's familiar black bag. They came in and went along with Bourke to the flatlet.

There were no introductions. The doctor looked at Blake and his wrist. 'The position with me is this,' said the doctor to Blake. 'You have a broken wrist. The normal procedure is that you should go to a hospital and have it set. However, for some reason I understand that you are allergic to hospitals. You refuse, in fact, to go to a hospital. Now, obviously you cannot go about with a broken wrist, and therefore I as a doctor consider it my duty to help you. This, I take it, is understood!'

'Yes, indeed,' said Blake, 'perfectly understood. And I appreciate it very much.'

'Good,' said the doctor. He went to the table where his bag was and opened it. 'I think it only fair I should tell you,' he went on, 'that it is at least ten years since I performed this particular operation.' The

[87]

doctor was clearly an honest man, no quack but a highly intelligent medico and also, as might perhaps be expected, a member of the CND.

The doctor turned to Bourke. 'I shall need some hot water for the plaster,' he said, 'and if you've got some newspapers we can use them to cover this table.' The only papers Bourke had were the morning ones, and these he spread out on the table oblivious that Blake's photographs were uppermost. But the doctor did not appear to notice them as Bourke brought a can of hot water from the bathroom and put it in the middle of the table.

'I shall give you a local anæsthetic,' the doctor told Blake. 'It may not kill all the pain but it will help.' He then took out of his bag the equipment needed for the operation – a hypodermic needle, anæsthetic, a tin of plaster and bandages. Bourke then took him into the bathroom next door where he thoroughly washed his hands and arms to the elbows with soap, scrubbing each finger and removing any dirt which might be under his nails. Bourke gave him a clean towel and held the door open since he was obviously determined not to touch anything before he handled his instruments.

First, while Bourke held Blake's arm steady, the doctor inserted the needle into the middle of the fracture, between the broken ends of the bone, which he then manipulated into line, pulling the ends apart. The anæsthetic only acted to a limited extent, since the sweat was pouring down Blake's face and he was writhing with pain. 'I think that's back in position all right now,' the doctor said when he had finished. Certainly the wrist looked straight again. Then the doctor opened the tin of plaster and emptied the white powder into the can of hot water, dipping the bandages into the liquid and winding them round Blake's wrist, forearm and hand, leaving only the fingers free. The same sling was used. 'The plaster should be hard in a couple of hours,' the doctor said, and added that to prevent any chance of infection he would give Blake a shot of penicillin which he proceeded to do, taking another needle from his bag. At Bourke's request he also produced some phials of sleeping powder. 'One per person per night,' he instructed.

Michael Reynolds looked at his watch and switched on the television, just in time to see the nine o'clock news. Again the escape was the first item. Blake's photograph appeared on the screen, followed by pictures of Wormwood Scrubs and diagrams showing the escape route.

The doctor glanced briefly at the screen, but although by this time he was almost certainly aware of his patient's identity, he gave no sign of recognition except for a faint smile. He then went out again to the bathroom, and while he was there Bourke asked Michael whether it would be all right to offer a fee. 'I don't think so,' Michael replied. 'It might be misinterpreted, and he is not that sort of a doctor.'

The doctor reappeared and was thanked profusely by Bourke and Blake. After he had left, Michael and his wife, and another friend, Pat Porter, who had offered to accommodate Blake when he had to leave Highlever Road, joined in an appropriate celebration of the occasion with a plethora of drinks. It was nearly midnight when they departed.

'We are very lucky men to know people like them,' Bourke remarked after they had gone.

'My friend,' said Blake, 'you don't have to remind me.'

7

All was quiet on Monday 24 October 1966, in the Highlever Road district. Bourke went out to buy food, also the newspapers, which were still full of the escape story. One possible clue was highlighted, the pot of chrysanthemums which Bourke had discarded at the scene of the escape, and it was given a mysterious significance, although the press and the security authorities did not realize that it was merely used as a cover for Bourke's walkie-talkie. Then the BBC programme *The World At One* came out with the extraordinary theory that Blake had never been in the prison at all, his trial was a mock one, a substitute went to Wormwood Scrubs while Blake lived elsewhere under an assumed name at the expense of MI6, the idea being that he should eventually go to Moscow, ostensibly working for the KGB but really for the British secret service. The same afternoon the Home Secretary Roy Jenkins announced that he had appointed Earl Mountbatten of Burma to head an official inquiry into prison security, with particular reference to the escape of George Blake. But this was not good enough for the Tory Opposition which tabled a censure motion. At the same time it was announced that all the other spies in Britain's gaols had been switched to new locations and were all in top-security prisons.

It was obvious that Blake could not stay much longer in Highlever Road since the flatlet was swept on Wednesdays by the landlady and the bed linen changed. On the Tuesday Michael phoned to say that he had found alternative accommodation for Blake but there was one small spare room and it could only take one of them. Michael arrived at 8 pm and apologized for this 'bad news'. But Bourke was not in the least disconcerted. 'I'm quite safe here,' he said, 'until they start publishing my photograph in the papers and on television.' He added that the police would not do this until they were convinced that he knew they were looking for him.

Michael went on to say that of course he would try to get Bourke fixed up as soon as he could. Then, speaking to Blake, he said: 'These people you're going to know who you are. They are worried about one thing. They are no more anxious than the rest of us to help Russian intelligence, and they'd like some sort of assurance that you're not going to pass on any more information.'

Blake had no difficulty in giving this assurance. 'I can assure you this question does not arise,' he said. 'Even if I wanted to pass on any more information, I couldn't, because I possess none. Any scraps of intelligence I might still have known at the time of my arrest would now be quite useless. So, you see, you need have no worries on that score.'

They then all went out to Michael's car. Michael and Anne got into the front seat, while Blake with an eye-patch and hat climbed into the back with the suitcase Bourke had bought him. The car moved off in the direction of central London, while Bourke returned to the flatlet and lay on the bed thinking. He did not like the idea of Blake being out of his sight, while it would only be a matter of time, perhaps a few days, before Scotland Yard issued his own name and photograph. Why not speed up the process? So he argued to himself. Scotland Yard's concentration on him would divert attention from Blake and make his hiding place safer.

Bourke then got up and left the house, walking to Latimer Road station and catching an underground train to Paddington. In the main-line station he noticed a police constable and a man in civvies, obviously a detective, who after giving him a searching glance looked at the passengers leaving a train which had just arrived. They were probably searching for someone, perhaps himself, Bourke thought.

Near the platform Bourke found a row of telephone booths. Putting on his gloves, he entered the first one and dialled Whitehall 1212. 'New Scotland Yard' was the immediate answer. Bourke asked to leave a message.

Told by the man at the switchboard that they could not take messages, Bourke asked to be put through to a police officer, any police officer.

After a short pause another voice came on the line, announcing his extension, and asking if he could help.

Satisfied that he was a policeman and had pen and paper handy, Bourke began: 'Start writing . . . The getaway car which took George Blake from Wormwood Scrubs . . .'

The policeman began to repeat Bourke's words very slowly, and Bourke guessed that he was reaching for another telephone. 'Now, look here,' Bourke broke in. 'I know you are trying to trace this call but you're wasting your time. The car is parked in Harvist Road, NW6.'

'Any identification?'

'Yes,' said Bourke, '117 GMX. Good night.' With that Bourke replaced the receiver and left the booth. He felt that Scotland Yard suspected that the escape had been carried out with the help of the criminal underworld, and that one of its members had betrayed him in revenge for some grievance, perhaps because he had not received his share of the loot in the form of money paid to secure Blake's release, the money of course coming from the Russians. On returning to Highlever Road, Bourke poured himself a stiff whisky and congratulated himself on having fooled the Yard.

On Thursday 27 October the car number was announced on

television. The police were also quoted as saying that they were anxious to trace the owner. They did not mention him by name, although of course they knew his identity since the vehicle had been registered in Bourke's name at his old address in Perryn Road.

Next day Michael phoned the flatlet and told Bourke he had found him a place to go to. It was a house in Cromwell Road, near Gloucester Road underground station. Michael and his wife took Bourke there the same evening, letting themselves in with Michael's key. The owner was away for the weekend, but Michael had spoken to him on the telephone and he said it would be all right. His mother was an old lady also living in the house and was expecting Bourke and Blake, though she had no idea who they were and did not watch television. Anne put a carrier bag on the bedroom floor. 'This is some food for you, Seán,' she said. 'It should keep you going until your hosts come back.' Bourke thanked her, and Michael handed him the key, and they said good night.

Next door there was a comfortable sitting room with a television, which Bourke switched on at news time. Photographs of Bourke's car were shown, while the announcer said that Scotland Yard knew the identity of the owner but was not prepared to divulge it. The announcer added that he was believed to be a thirty-two-year-old Irishman.

Next day Bourke arrived, having had a dreadful stay at his previous hideout where the residents insisted that he stayed in bed, gave him a bucket for his natural functions and would not let him go to the bathroom and empty it until one o'clock in the morning.

Blake was interested to be in Cromwell Road since, as he observed, he used to work not far away in this road when he was with MI6 in London. But they did not stay very long there since it appeared that their host's wife was undergoing psychiatric treatment and she had told her psychiatrist that two men on the run from the police were staying in the house, although she mentioned no names. Michael therefore decided they should move, and it was arranged that Bourke should go back temporarily to Highlever Road while Blake went to Pat Porter's flat in Hampstead. Meanwhile on Monday 31 October, the Labour Government defeated the Opposition motion of censure by a substantial majority, Roy Jenkins distinguishing himself by his speech and the Prime Minister assuring the House that Blake no longer constituted a threat to Britain's security. The same evening as the debate was reported, Bourke's identity was disclosed and his former landlady in Perryn Road was interviewed. Asked what her tenant was like, she replied: 'He was really quite a nice man, always smartly dressed and well spoken. However, he kept himself very much to himself. But he was not the sort of man you would expect to get mixed up in anything like this. He left here and said he was going to Ireland. Later on I got a card from him.' Bourke's mother agreed with this when she was seen at her home in Limerick by two Special Branch officers. 'I can't understand it,' she was quoted by one paper as saying. 'My son is a good boy. He wouldn't do a thing like that.'

Blake was anxious that Bourke should join him, which he did on 7 November at Pat Porter's flat. Here he had a room to himself instead of having to share one with Blake. Four days later, Friday 11 November, was Blake's birthday, and they had a congenial party, joined by their host as well as Michael and Anne Reynolds. Funds were running low and the question of Blake leaving Britain was discussed on this occasion and at other meetings when Michael and Anne joined them for meals. Blake was not anxious at first to go to an Iron Curtain country. Egypt was his favourite choice, which he remembered well from his young days and where he still had friends and relations. Michael thought that he might be unsure of his reception in the Soviet Union. This may well have been the case, since the Russians were surprised by his escape and thought the Czechs had something to do with it, since he had on occasion supplied the Czech authorities with secret intelligence. MI5, like the general public, assumed that the Russians had financed Blake's escape, although MI5's interception of Soviet communications by telephone tapping and such like showed that the Russians were quite surprised at the operation and disclaimed any direct knowledge of it.

It was eventually decided that Blake should go to East Germany as he spoke German fluently and Berlin was the closest point from which to cross into Eastern Europe.

As for Seán Bourke, he was for going to Ireland and fighting any demands for his extradition on the grounds that his offence in 'springing' Blake from prison was 'political'. But the others were against this, arguing that since Blake was a Communist, who had spied for Russia against Britain, he could not expect much sympathy from an anti-Communist country which was economically dependent upon Britain. Hence Bourke consented with some reluctance to follow Blake at a later date, but he also said that he would only stay with him for a short time.

During their time in Hampstead, Bourke had some passport photographs taken of himself. He then met an ex-prisoner friend in a pub off Tottenham Court Road, who promised to get him a false passport. He received it within twenty-four hours, made out in the name of James Richardson, British subject and architect, of Oxford Gardens, London, NW10.

Bourke showed Blake the passport which Blake examined carefully. 'Speaking as a former Vice-Consul, one of whose tasks was to issue these things,' he remarked as he handed it back, 'I can assure you it is an excellent job.'

The remaining funds were used to buy a second-hand Dormobile, in which Blake would be driven to East Germany. Bourke offered to drive himself, but Michael pointed out the dangers of this ploy. If Bourke were recognized, he said, Blake's discovery would be automatic since the vehicle would be literally torn apart. Michael then said he would drive himself and Anne intervened to say she would come along too to make her husband look even more respectable. Blake, as usual, was profuse in his thanks for the risk they were taking. 'It's the only way it can be done,' said Michael.

Saturday 17 December was settled as the date for departure. The Dormobile was fitted with a kitchen unit and a bed. As the result of some structural changes Michael and his wife made to the bed and the dependent drawer designed for storing blankets and linen, there was a cavity large enough to hold Blake in a cramped position with the addition of a sheet of foam rubber to make his position a little more comfortable. The route chosen was the Dover ferry to Ostend, across Belgium and West Germany to the East German border, then by the Berlin autobahn to a point on East German territory outside Berlin where Blake would be dropped. Michael and Anne would go on to West Berlin and spend a day or two there before returning to England by the same route.

They all had dinner together on the evening of the Saturday departure date. Blake took the opportunity to ask Bourke when he expected to follow 'so I can tell them you are coming and they can be waiting for you'. Bourke had already looked up the times of suitable trains and flights, which he had noted on a piece of paper from which he read. 'I shall leave here exactly two weeks after you, on New Year's Eve,' he said. 'I shall take the London/Paris night train which leaves Victoria at nine o'clock and is due at the Gare du Nord in Paris at eight o'clock the following morning. From there I shall take a taxi to Orly airport and catch a plane to West Berlin. I shall spend one night there and cross over to East Berlin through Checkpoint Charlie at ten o'clock on Monday morning, the second of January.'

'Well, that sounds easy enough,' said Blake. 'Provided your passport is in order you should have no difficulty. I know from experience that crossing from West Berlin to East Berlin is not a problem. In fact, anyone holding the passport of any of the occupying nations is entitled under the Potsdam Agreement to travel freely between the two Berlins.'

Before Blake left, Michael produced a brown paper parcel which he unwrapped to reveal a rubber hot-water bottle. 'You will be hidden in that compartment for a long time,' he told Blake. 'From here to Dover and certainly all the way across in the ferry to Ostend. Nine or ten hours at least. In case nature should make an untimely demand, it will be useful to have this.' Before handing it to Blake, he unscrewed the top and inserted his forefinger in the hole. 'I hope it's the right size,' he said to the accompaniment of laughter from his wife, though the remark made Blake blush.

So they took off after affectionate farewells to Seán Bourke and Pat Porter. The two left behind listened to all the news bulletins, but there was no mention of Blake during the next forty-eight hours. When Pat came back from work on the Monday evening, he looked pleased. 'They've made it,' he said excitedly. 'They've bloody well made it! Michael phoned me this afternoon from West Berlin.'

When Michael and Anne got back in January 1967, they recounted the details of the journey. Everything went off without a hitch. There was no trouble at the various frontier customs including the East German. The worst thing was the delays at Dover and Ostend when the boat was a couple of hours late in leaving Dover and there was another hour's hold-up at Ostend before they could drive off. It took a further hour before they thought it safe to let Blake out. He had been inside for twelve hours, and Anne was afraid that he might have been suffocated. But he was in reasonably good shape and had used the hot-water bottle.

'We thought the East Germans were bound to look in the Dormobile at the frontier post,' said Michael. 'But they didn't look at all. We drove on and dropped George off on the autobahn about a mile from an East German guard post just outside Berlin. George told us that he would give us time to reach the city before giving himself up to the East Germans. We drove into Berlin, stayed a couple of days and then came back. And even when we were *leaving* East Germany the Dormobile wasn't searched.'

Pat Porter was keen on going to the flatlet in Highlever Road, and recovering Bourke's belongings there, although these were not of any great value – a typewriter, the two walkie-talkies, a tape recorder and a few books. Bourke vainly reasoned with him, pointing out that the police might have discovered its whereabouts and were watching it in case he should return. Bourke was determined that Pat should not turn up there, since he would not only be endangering his own liberty but that of Michael and Anne. To forestall this possibility, on 30 December he posted a photograph of himself to a newspaper with '28 Highlever Road, W10' scrawled on the back of the photograph in another hand. It was very likely, as indeed happened, that the newspaper would immediately inform Scotland Yard, but by that time Bourke reckoned he would be safely out of the country. This is what happened.

When the police arrived, the landlady told them that Mr Sigsworth had not been there for some time on account of his roving commission as a journalist, but the rent had been regularly paid to date by postal order. The police had no difficulty in identifying fingerprints in the flatlet as those of Seán Bourke, although they

Henry Curiel, founder of the Egyptian Communist Party and Blake's uncle. Blake spent a year with him in Cairo as a youth and was ideologically influenced by him. Curiel was assassinated aged 63 by right-wing extremists in Paris, May 1982.

TOP

Blake and fellow prisoners arriving at RAF Abingdon from Korea, April 1953. (From left) Blake, Bishop Cooper, Commissioner Lord, Consul Owen, Monsignor Quinlan.

BOTTOM

Sir Vyvyan Holt, British Minister in Seoul, interned with Blake for three years in North Korea, 1950-53.

TOP
The secret tunnel in Berlin which Blake betrayed to the Russians.

BOTTOM
George Blake at the time of his arrest in 1961.

TOP

East wall of Wormwood Scrubs Prison looking south along Artillery Road. The bollards were placed outside the wall after Blake's escape.

BOTTOM

Nikita Sergeyevich Khrushchev, Soviet Communist Party First Secretary and Prime Minister during the period that Blake was spying for the Russians. He fell from power in October 1964 and died in September 1971, aged 77.

TOP
Manuscript of Bourke's book showing deletions made by the KGB.

MIDDLE
Seán Alphonsus Bourke at the time of his arrest in 1961.

BOTTOM
Seán Bourke at work on his book *The Springing of George Blake* in Blake's Moscow flat.

TOP

The Ambassador Sir David Kelly and his wife on the balcony of the British embassy in Moscow, with the Kremlin in the background.

BOTTOM

Konon Molody, alias Gordon Lonsdale, reading a congenial book on his profession. Sentenced in 1961 to 25 years for espionage, he was exchanged in April 1964 for the British agent Greville Wynne, who was being held in Moscow.

TOP
Blake on holiday with his mother in the Soviet Union during her second visit in 1968.
BOTTOM
Blake with his mother in Moscow in April 1967.

TOP

Picnic luncheon at Kim Philby's dacha outside Moscow. Philby (in white shirt) is talking to his fifth wife Nina, a Russian. Blake is on the right with his second wife Ida, also a Russian, and their son Mischa.

BOTTOM

KGB Headquarters in Dzerzhinsky Square in Moscow. Blake is the figure with his back to the camera. The dreaded Lubyanka prison is at the rear of the building.

could find no others since Bourke had been careful to wipe all the furniture carefully.

Many years later, in April 1983, when Kenneth de Courcy deposited his private papers in the Hoover Institution at Stanford University, California, the archivist asked him whether the account of the escape which Bourke had written in *The Springing of George Blake* (1970) was accurate, as far as he knew.

'As far as I know, from inside the prison, yes,' de Courcy replied.

There were lots of things in his account, of course, which I didn't know until he told me. I didn't know who paid for it, for example. It was he who told me that the Campaign for Nuclear Disarmament paid. It was he who told me how much it cost – £600. It was he who told me that Blake had broken his wrist going over the wall. And it was he who told me that he was at a house only a mile-and-a-half from the prison; and it was a CND doctor who had treated his wrist. And it was he who told me that Blake's excuse for going to Russia – which he always told all his friends that he would never dream of doing – was that the £600 was running out and that they had no more money . . .

He was smuggled right across the East German frontier. Then there was quite a problem explaining to the Russian authorities that he really was George Blake. They hadn't organized his escape . . . So it was quite a business to persuade them this really was entrepreneur George.

'That's Bourke's story,' de Courcy continued. 'I wasn't there.' But he *was* in Wormwood Scrubs at the time of the escape, and the last occasion on which he saw Blake was about an hour before that event when Blake gave him a book which de Courcy still possesses and which he showed the present writer. It was Blake's own copy of the Koran in the original Arabic which he had used in his language studies.

To be strictly accurate, the two former members of the CND who had joined the militant Committee of 100, Michael Reynolds and Pat Porter, raised the necessary funds, and made the arrangements for supplies, accommodation and travel. But Bourke seems to have regarded the CND and the Committee of 100 as more or less synonymous. Today, since Bertrand Russell's death in 1970, the Committee of 100 has become virtually non-existent, while the CND continues to flourish.

3

In Soviet Russia with the KGB

I

CERTAINLY George Blake did have some difficulty in convincing the Soviet authorities of his identity when he arrived in East Germany which he did on 19 December 1966. It will be recalled that Michael Reynolds had dropped him near an East German guard post on the Berlin *autobahn*. Blake walked into the guard post to find its occupants surprised to see a foreign stranger. They tried to make him tell them who he was, but Blake refused and asked to see a Russian officer. Eventually, after some argument, they telephoned the Soviet sector in Berlin and an hour later a Russian officer arrived. It was now two o'clock in the morning. Blake told him who he was and the officer said he would have to return to his headquarters at Karlshorst and report there, since he was not in a position to confirm Blake's identification. Before leaving, the officer instructed the Germans in the guard post to fix up the visitor with a bed.

At nine o'clock in the morning three Russians came into the room where Blake was sleeping. The one in the middle was a man with whom Blake had been in contact when he had been working in Berlin years before. The officer immediately recognized Blake and threw his arms round him, exclaiming, 'It's him! It's him!' The officer had actually been asleep in Moscow when the KGB received a call asking for someone to identify the stranger in the guard post. During the ensuing six hours the identifying officer had been woken up, rushed to a military airfield outside Moscow, flown to East Berlin and driven to the guard post – an efficient performance which impressed Blake.

Blake was taken to the Soviet *Kommandtura*, where he was lodged for several days in charge of two KGB officers, Vladimir who had the rank of Lieutenant-Colonel and Edmund who was a Major. They lived in one of the houses in the compound surrounded by Soviet soldiers with machine guns at the ready. From there Blake was flown to Moscow, landing in a military airfield about thirty miles south of the capital. There he was warmly welcomed by the Soviet authorities and installed in a comfortable flat with a cook-housekeeper called Zinaida Ivanova to do his shopping and look after him generally. Zinaida was helped by her daughter Sofia, a buxom girl of twenty-five who worked during the day as a translator at the Ministry of Foreign Trade, helping her mother with the cooking in the evenings and sharing her room in the flat.

Seán Bourke left London as arranged, arriving in West Berlin on New Year's Day 1967 and spending the night at the Zoo Hotel in the Kurfurstendamm. He pretended to be a tourist anxious to see as much of the divided city as possible and asked the hall porter about the procedure for getting to and through Checkpoint Charlie. He negotiated the border on his false passport as he had done at the other frontier checkpoints. He then began to walk along the street and after a short distance he passed a stationary black car by the kerb facing the same direction as he was walking. The car engine started up and the vehicle passed him but stopped a little further on. Bourke was about to pass it for the second time when the rear door opened and a man leaned out. He was wearing a grey overcoat and a matching fur hat.

'Mr Richardson?' the man asked.

'Yes,' said Bourke, stopping.

'Please get in,' said the man in the fur hat. He moved to the far side as Bourke entered. When the door was closed the car moved off at speed, while the other man smiled broadly. 'Well, Mr Bourke,' he said. 'I would have recognized you anywhere. George gave us a very good description of you.' As they shook hands the man added, 'By the way, my name is Vladimir.' It was the same KGB colonel who had met Blake.

Henceforth, Bourke was told, he would be known as Robert Adamovich Garvin, the patronymic being explained to him by Vladimir, who also told him, after he had telephoned the Moscow comrades, that since Bourke was only wearing a thin suit and a crumpled mac, he would need some warm clothes. In due course these arrived in two suitcases, on which Vladimir had been authorized to spend 2,000 DM. 'If you went to Moscow in your own clothes,' said Vladimir, 'you would literally freeze to death.' Bourke was to be glad of the fur coat, fur hat and fur boots.

The KGB colonel Vladimir accompanied him on the flight to the same military airfield south of Moscow where Blake had landed and where they were met by a young KGB man called Victor who drove with them to the city. There their car pulled up outside a rather old-fashioned hotel, the Leningradskaya, opposite the railway station for Leningrad, a mile or so north-east of the Kremlin on the edge of the inner city. 'This is where you will stay for the time being,' Vladimir told him. Then the colonel and Victor took Bourke's suitcases out of the boot and passing through the hotel's swing doors carried them up to Bourke's room on the second floor. It was a small room with old-fashioned furniture, including a green-topped desk with an ornate brass lamp and a blotter, also a telephone. Vladimir then said good-bye and expressed his hope that he and Bourke would meet again, after which he handed him over to Victor's charge.

After Vladimir had left, Victor picked up the phone, dialled a number and spoke briefly in Russian. Then, turning to Bourke, he said, 'We shall now go and meet George for lunch.' Victor led the way downstairs where they waited for a few minutes inside the swing doors. Suddenly, a man entered, and seeing Victor came over. He was a tall, lean, broad-shouldered KGB officer of about forty. 'Mr Bourke,' he smiled as he shook hands. 'An excellent operation. Welcome to Moscow.' He then introduced himself as Stanislav, adding that his friends called him Stan and he hoped Bourke would do the same. 'Well, let's go,' he said, pointing at the swing doors.

Outside a chauffeur-driven car was waiting for them and they got into it. Bourke noted that they drove to the end of Kalanchevskaya Street, where the hotel was located, turned left and a little later turned right, drawing up at a block of flats behind the shops that lined that street. Getting out, Stan led the way up a flight of concrete steps to the landing on the third floor. Stan then pressed the doorbell three times, pausing after each ring. Eventually the door was unlocked, and a grey-haired woman peeped out. As soon as she saw Stan she let them in. She was Blake's housekeeper Zinaida, Stan explained, as she took their hats and coats. Blake was in his study off the dining room, sitting behind a highly polished mahogany desk. He was dressed in a dark new suit and looked much better than when Bourke had last seen him in London. 'Well,' he said as they shook hands, 'I am very glad to see you,' to which Bourke replied smiling, 'We made it then.'

There followed the celebration lunch, with borshch, various kinds of meat, cabbage, chicken and ham, plenty of wine, vodka and Armenian brandy. Zinaida waited on them. Blake proposed the first toast: 'To Seán, without whose courage and ingenuity we would not be here this afternoon!' During the meal, which lasted for two hours, it appeared that Stan, who wore a well-cut English suit, had been the KGB man in the Soviet Embassy in London for a couple of years, hence his excellent English. He had been to Moscow University and qualified as a lawyer before joining the KGB, where he now had the rank of Lieutenant-Colonel. Victor, too had been to Moscow University, and had graduated in history. He had only recently joined the KGB. After Victor left, the other three adjourned to Blake's study with another bottle of brandy. During their talk there, Stan remarked that he had gathered that Bourke had edited the prison magazine in Wormwood Scrubs and, if he was interested, he would get him something in that line such as correcting the English translations from the Russian in Soviet publishing houses. Bourke said he was agreeable and was told that it would not be necessary for him to go to the publishing offices but that Stan or Victor would collect the manuscripts and Bourke could work in his room at the hotel. Stan then got up to go expecting to take Bourke with him, but Blake said he would walk Bourke back to his hotel. This he did, and after they exchanged telephone numbers they arranged to meet next day, which was Sunday.

Accordingly Victor, who had been assigned as a general guide, collected them both, telling them that there was a very good view of Moscow from the Lenin Hills and he thought they should go there. They were not really hills but sloping land at the western edge of the city dominated by Moscow University. There happened to be some cars parked near the wall, two of which bore diplomatic numbers, so Victor moved on to prevent them being seen by the foreign embassy staff in their care.

Two days later, on Tuesday evening, Blake telephoned Bourke at his hotel and invited him to dinner. 'I've got something interesting to show you,' he said. 'A little surprise.' When Bourke accepted the invitation Blake arranged to meet him outside the Ministry of Transport, 'the big building at the top of the street where your hotel is'. They duly met and trudged through the snow to Blake's flat.

The dinner table was set for four as before. 'This time,' Blake explained, 'I have decided to invite Zinaida and her daughter to join us.' He then went into his bedroom, opened the wardrobe and took out the insignia of two orders which he pinned to his suit.

In response to Bourke's question, Blake pointed at one, 'The Order of Lenin,' he announced proudly. 'It was presented to me at a special lunch yesterday by the Minister of State Security on behalf of the Soviet Government.' The Minister, it is of interest to note, was Vladimir Yemifovich Semichastny, the youngest man ever to be appointed head of the KGB, which he was in 1961, being a protégé of his predecessor Alexander Shelepin and like him a former member of the Young Communist League. His appointment confirmed that the KGB was once again under the control of the Soviet Communist Party after the Beria era when it competed with it for power. But as an appointee of Khrushchev his position had to some extent been undermined by Khrushchev's loss of power two years previously, added to which, as will be seen, he was responsible for some embarrassing incidents which displeased the Politburo and was eventually to result in his dismissal. But these had nothing to do with Blake or any of the British double agents.

The other decoration which Blake proudly showed off was the Military Order of the Red Banner which among others Kim Philby and Guy Burgess had been awarded. Zinaida and her daughter were so impressed by Blake's awards that he was persuaded to wear them during dinner, as he sat at the head of the table looking distinctly pleased with himself. As at the earlier dinner there were several toasts including one 'to Seán, without whom we would not be here tonight'.

For the next fortnight or so Bourke dined at Blake's flat nearly every day. On one occasion, when Stan joined them, Blake suggested that Bourke should move into the flat. 'After all, Stan,' he pointed out, 'this is quite a large flat and Seán could have the study. The couch in there makes a bed, and Zinaida could as easily cook for two of us as for one. And it would save you all the trouble of having to send Victor to the Leningradskaya every day to interpret for him.'

'It's not a bad idea,' Stan agreed, 'but I would have to get permission from my chief.'

The permission from Semichastny was forthcoming and Bourke duly moved into the flat. A few days later Stan appeared looking very worried. 'Seán,' he began, 'I'm afraid I have some bad news for you.'

'Oh, what is it?'

'Your flatlet at Highlever Road has been discovered by Scotland Yard, and you have now been publicly named as the man wanted for questioning.' It will be recalled that Bourke himself was responsible for this in order to prevent Pat Porter from going there to recover his few belongings, possibly leaving fingerprints.

'Well, it was bound to happen sooner or later,' said Bourke, feeling relieved.

'But it is a pity that it had to happen at all,' said Stan, pacing up and down the room and looking thoughtful. 'This changes your position radically.'

'I don't see how it changes anything,' Bourke retorted. 'I have always considered it inevitable that my identity would become known to the police, and my intention has always been to return to Ireland and fight extradition.'

'But, Seán, George is a Communist and Ireland is a Catholic country. Ireland is also economically dependent on Britain. Laws can be given different interpretations to suit the convenience of Governments. And there would be a great deal of pressure on the Irish Government if you were to go back there.'

'That's a chance I'll have to take,' said Bourke. 'And anyway we've gained something from this development. Now the police know that I am the culprit they will be concentrating on looking for me, and their net will be spread much less wide. So my friends will have an even greater chance of escaping detection.'

George Blake agreed wholeheartedly, pointing out that Michael Reynolds and Pat Porter were not known criminals; nor were they known to be friends of Seán Bourke. 'The police will now concentrate on his known friends,' he went on nodding in Bourke's direction, 'including those he had known in prison, and thus Michael and Pat should be in the clear. As I see it, this discovery and Seán's established guilt are a blessing. It is the best thing that could have happened from the point of view of our friends in London.'

'Yes, you may have a point there,' Stan conceded.

'When will you see the papers?' asked Bourke.

'I'll get a cable off to London for them tomorrow,' Stan promised.

A few days later the newspapers arrived and sure enough Seán Bourke's photograph was on the front pages. MAN WHO HELPED BLAKE STILL IN LONDON was a banner headline in one paper accompanied by a photograph of Bourke taken at the time of his trial in Sussex in 1961.

'Well,' said Stan, 'since they believe you are still in London, let's keep it that way. When you want to write to your family we'll send the letters to London in the diplomatic bag and have them posted there.' Blake's were already being posted by the same means in Cairo.

2

Seán Bourke was given a test as a translator by a Moscow firm of publishers with results which amused both Blake and Stan. His task was to correct the translation of an article which had appeared in a Soviet magazine. It was about a heroic Russian woman worker named Ekaterina Borisovna, who was manager of a collective farm and also a member of the local Soviet. One passage in the article, describing the activities on the farm was rendered:

The many-voiced hubbub of a thousand white hens filled the huge barn, their red cocks swaying in the wind.

When he read this Bourke penned the following characteristic note at the bottom of the page:

In English, *cock* is a slang word for the male sexual organ, or penis. Therefore, to talk of the hens with their 'red cocks swaying in the wind' is to suggest that Ekaterina Borisovna kept some strange birds. On the other hand, *cock* is also an abbreviation of *cockerel*, the male bird of the species; but it is difficult to imagine why these sturdy creatures should sway in the wind unless, of course, they were drunk. I think the word you are looking for is probably *comb*.

On the strength of this effort, Bourke was accepted for the job. His first – and, as it happened his only work to correct – was entitled *Scientific Communism – A Popular Outline* and written by a Russian professor of political science in the university. It, like the other, contained some amusing sentences such as 'The power of man's muscle, wind and water was gradually replaced by electricity.'

The KGB paid Bourke 300 roubles a month, whether he worked or not. As the exchange rate was two-and-a-half roubles to the pound, Bourke thus got the equivalent of nearly £30 a week, in addition to his board and accommodation in Blake's flat, so that he was quite comfortably provided for compared with the wages of the average worker in a factory, shop or collective farm. He could also buy any delicacies he fancied in the stores which only accepted foreign currency.

Stan would come to the flat every day to collect Bourke's work and also the memoranda on the British secret service and other topics which Blake was writing for the KGB. Stan also used a tape recorder to record Blake's conversations with him and answers to his questions which took place in Blake's bedroom. About twice a week Stan would take them both to a restaurant for dinner, avoiding those frequented by westerners. On the way back in the car Stan would be dropped off at various addresses, since he was divorced and had a lot of women friends. Bourke liked him, noting that he was the nearest thing to the James Bond image that he had encountered in the Soviet Union.

On the other hand, Seán Bourke soon regretted that he had left the Leningradskaya hotel so readily for Blake's flat. The reason was that Blake's manner towards him had changed completely. Instead of the patient and sympathetic character Bourke had known at Wormwood Scrubs, Blake had become intolerant, arrogant and even ruthless. 'I risked my liberty to save him from life-long imprisonment,' Bourke was later to write, 'and he repaid me with treachery. The George Blake that we had all known at Wormwood Scrubs had never really existed. It had been an elaborate and calculated pose with a long-term objective. In Moscow, with no more reason for posing, George Blake reverted to type.'

From the outset Blake was determined to let Bourke know that the flat was his and it was a privilege he had bestowed upon Bourke to allow him to live there. Also, he insisted on addressing Bourke as Robert, although Stan always called him Seán. Nor did Blake miss any opportunity to assert his superiority. He hated noise, or at least said he did. Once when Bourke was sitting in the study listening to some music on the BBC World Service, Blake burst into the room, saying, 'Robert, would you mind turning the radio down a bit, it's impossible for me to concentrate.' The radio was already on low volume, but Bourke obligingly turned it down so that it became practically inaudible. But this did not satisfy Blake who appeared five minutes later and asked Bourke to turn the radio off, saying 'it is quite impossible for me to write'. Bourke did so.

The housekeeper and her daughter were similarly treated. One evening Blake strode into the kitchen while the two women were there with Bourke. Blake first spoke in Russian and when Bourke noted that they seemed upset by what Blake had said, he then turned to Bourke. 'Having made my announcement in Russian,' he said, 'I shall now translate it into English. With effect from today all noise and all movement in this flat are to cease by eleven o'clock at night at the very latest. I do not consider it at all unreasonable that I should be allowed to sleep by eleven o'clock. I cannot do this if people are walking about and making a noise. That is all I wish to say. Good night!' With that he left the kitchen and went to his bedroom.

Zinaida Ivanova then said something to her daughter which Sofia interpreted since her mother could not speak English. 'My mother and I are thinking of leaving and going back to our own flat,' said Sofia. 'My mother can then come and do the cooking each day and go home at night.' However, they did not leave, fearing to displease the KGB since whenever Stan appeared they used to go off into their bedroom and stay there until he had left, sometimes by himself and sometimes with the other two for dinner in a restaurant.

It was at this time, in April 1967, that the KGB chief Vladimir Semichastny was dismissed after a reign of a little more than six years. Semichastny had made a number of serious mistakes. One was to sanction the arrest as a spy of a Yale University professor, Frederick Barghoorn, the object being to use the professor, who was visiting Moscow, as a hostage in exchange for the Soviet spy Igor Ivanov who had been caught red-handed by the FBI in New York. Unfortunately for Semichastny, Barghoorn was a close friend of President Kennedy, who established at a press conference that he was in no way involved in espionage and demanded the release of the innocent professor, to which the humiliated KGB Chief was obliged to accede. What immediately led to his dismissal was his failure to supervise the movements of Stalin's daughter Svetlana and let her defect to the United States from India. Semichastny's successor was the Politburo's hatchetman Yuri Vladimirovich Andropov, who was to last for fifteen years as boss of the Lubyanka and end up as President of the Soviet Union. He had previously served as Soviet ambassador in Budapest and was intimately concerned with the harsh suppression of the Hungarian rising in 1966. One of his achievements as the new KGB Chief was to establish psychiatric hospitals on the ground that dissidents and anyone else who questioned the merits of Soviet communism must be mad anyway. Andropov was also an expert in the craft of disinformation. 'The political role of the USSR,' he was quoted as saying, 'must be supported abroad by the dissemination of false news and provocative information.' At the same time he modernized the KGB's tactics without changing its aims, 'knocking the rough edges off the KGB' to give it a new and more attractive image, according to Kim Philby, whom Andropov is said to have consulted. However, these changes did not adversely affect either Blake or Bourke.

However, relations between the two progressively deteriorated during the next few months. One Sunday, for instance, when it had been arranged that Victor should take them out for a day in the country, Bourke entered the kitchen where he found Blake preparing sandwiches. 'This isn't easy, you know,' said Blake. 'I have to make sandwiches for the three of us and the driver too. It's a lot of work.'

'I'm sure it is,' Bourke agreed.

'So you think that's funny, do you?'

'Nobody said anything about being funny,' Bourke remarked.

'So you think it's funny, do you?' Blake repeated. 'Well, damn you!' He picked up a plastic container full of boiled eggs and threw it at Bourke, missing him by about two feet, while the container hit the wall and the eggs fell on the floor. He then picked up half-a-dozen apples from the kitchen table and proceeded to throw them, one after another against the wall. 'Damn you! Damn you! Damn you!' he kept screaming. He then ran off into his room, slamming the door loudly behind him. It was a most embarrassing scene, particularly as it was witnessed by Zinaida Ivanova and Sofia who were both in the kitchen. Victor arrived shortly afterwards, but Blake insisted on staying in his room for the rest of the day, leaving Bourke and Victor to make the trip without him.

Shortly after this incident a KGB man, with whom Blake worked in Britain and who knew that Bourke was sharing the flat nominally as Robert Garvin, called to see Blake. They talked for a while about old times, apparently in English, since Bourke was in the kitchen with the door ajar and overheard their conversation.

'And how is Robert?' the KGB man asked.

'Oh, he's not too bad.'

'And what are his plans?'

'Well, you see Robert is just . . . well . . . just an Irish peasant.

He doesn't know what he wants. That's the trouble. But anyway we're trying to condition him to stay here, to settle down in the Soviet Union. We're working at it.'

After the KGB man left, Blake came into the kitchen carrying a bottle of champagne and two glasses and said, as he habitually did when he was in a good mood, 'I say, Robert, what is your attitude to a glass of champagne?' So they drank the bottle together.

Bourke waited for a week before tackling Blake on his future, since he did not wish Blake to suspect that he had overheard what Blake had said about his being a peasant – incidentally quite untrue, since his forebears had been businessmen in Limerick and had no rustic or farming origins. 'Well,' said Bourke, 'I have now been in Moscow for more than three months and I think it's time I reminded Stan that my stay here is supposed to be temporary. I want to go back to Ireland.'

'And what about Michael and Pat?' queried Blake.

'What about them?'

'By returning to Ireland you would be putting them in danger.'

'Now look here,' said Bourke, 'it's *my* future we're discussing, not other people's. Michael and Pat are in no danger from me or from anyone else. I'm the one with the price on his head. I'm the one on the run, living in a strange country among strange people. I am already accepting the blame and drawing the police away from the others . . . but I'm not going to spend the rest of my life as a hunted man living in a country that I don't want to live in. I want to go back to Ireland and face extradition and return to a normal way of life. I want to be Seán Bourke, an Irishman, not Robert Garvin, a non-person. My future may not be important to you but it is very important to me.'

'Very well,' Blake said resentfully. 'I'll pass on your remarks to Stan.'

Whether he did so was not immediately apparent. Bourke decided to wait and see if Stan did raise the matter; but May, June and much of July passed without a hint from Stan about Bourke's future. Then Bourke was told that Blake's mother was arriving on 21 July to spend a month with her son and that the KGB chiefs had decided that she should not meet Bourke or find out that he was in Moscow.

To avoid this Bourke would be taken for a holiday on the Black Sea. Thus as Mrs Blake's plane was coming in to land at Moscow airport, Bourke's was taking off for the Caucasus, accompanied by a KGB officer named Slava with the same rank as Stan, a colonel. Slava took Bourke to Sochi, the most popular seaside resort on the shores of the Black Sea, with instructions to see that Bourke enjoyed himself. Since Mrs Blake wished to spend an extra week with her son, which she did partly in Moscow and partly at a holiday resort near the Polish border, Bourke did not return to Moscow until Saturday 26 August.

Victor was waiting for him at Moscow airport with a car and drove him to the flat where Blake was waiting, much better humoured than usual. When Bourke told him about the girls he met in Sochi, Blake exclaimed: 'My, my! It sounds like something out of the *Arabian Nights* or out of James Bond for that matter.'

'Just a month in the life of Seán Bourke,' was Bourke's laughing response. 'And how did you get on yourself?'

'We had a wonderful time,' said Blake. 'My mother enjoyed herself tremendously.' He then filled two glasses with brandy and handed Bourke one. 'By the way,' Blake went on, 'my mother was able to give me some very interesting information about the activities of the police while we were in London. The Special Branch were at her house within an hour of the escape. They asked her if she knew anything about it and she admitted straight away, of course, that you had asked her to finance the operation. A few days later an inspector flew out to Bangkok to talk to Adéle, and she confirmed my mother's story. So you see, they were on to you from the start.'

Bourke nodded as Blake went on: 'The Special Branch were furious with you. They did everything they could to discredit you in the hope that if anyone knew where you were hiding they would give you away. The inspector in charge of the investigation told my mother that you were an evil man and that you were likely to come back and try to blackmail her. That, in fact, was the explanation he gave for keeping a permanent watch on her house.'

'Coming from the police, that doesn't surprise me at all,' said Bourke, feeling that Blake spoke with an almost devilish sense of satisfaction.

'There is something else that will interest you, Robert,' Blake added as he sipped his drink. 'A book has been published about me called *Shadow of a Spy*. The last few chapters deal with the escape and you are named as the brains behind it. Just before publication extracts from it appeared for two weeks in the *Sunday Express*. Stan is going to bring the papers and the book on Monday.'

'I look forward to reading them' was Bourke's reaction to this news.

As Bourke was unpacking his suitcase, he came upon some photographs which he had taken some time before and which had been developed for him by his Russian teacher, a girl called Anna. They were quite ordinary photographs of Moscow and the surrounding countryside, some also taken by Victor showing Bourke and Blake together. But none of them was taken during Bourke's holiday in Sochi. They were wrapped in a towel and Bourke had forgotten about them. However, Blake caught sight of them as Bourke was taking them out of his case and he dashed across the room and snatched them from his hand. 'I haven't seen these have I? I had better have a look at them.' He took the pictures to his own room and returned them to Bourke next day with the terse comment that they had not come out very well.

Stan called two days later, on the Monday, with *Shadow of a Spy* and copies of the *Sunday Express*. As usual he first went to Blake's room where they talked at some length, beginning with a discussion of the book. Meanwhile Bourke was in the kitchen, boiling the kettle for some tea. The door to Blake's room was ajar and Bourke heard Stan ask Blake how Bourke had enjoyed his holiday. Blake replied that he said he had had a wonderful time, having wild parties at restaurants and going to bed with half a dozen girls. 'But that's probably a lot of lies,' he said.

'Oh, I don't think so,' replied Stan. 'I told the people in Sochi to lay everything on for him.'

Lowering his voice, Blake went on to tell Stan about the photographs, which he said he was sure Bourke did not have with him before he went on holiday. 'Do you think he made contact with someone from the West while he was in Sochi, got these photographs developed, and then passed on copies to this foreigner?'

There followed a few moments silence while Stan was obviously thinking. 'Well,' he said finally, 'I don't really think so.'

The kettle in the kitchen was now boiling and Bourke went over and made a pot of tea. Returning to where he had been standing near the door, he heard Blake say, 'I think that's the best idea. You'll go out and tell him yourself, will you?'

Bourke took the teapot with a cup and saucer into the study, where he sat down at his desk and poured himself some tea. A few minutes later there was a knock on the door and Stan came in. He looked troubled but was not unfriendly. He wasted no time at getting to the point.

'Seán,' he began, 'now that you have been in Moscow for eight months and the summer is over and you have had your holiday, you must be giving some thought to your future.'

'I seldom think of anything else.'

Stan hesitated before going on. 'Seán, we have been thinking about it too, and our conclusion is that you should stay in the Soviet Union for at least five years.'

Bourke was stunned by this announcement. It reminded him of the seven year sentence he had received from the judge at Sussex assizes. He looked flushed and angry. 'I'm sorry, Seán,' said Stan. 'Don't take it too badly.'

'How do you expect me to take it?' said Bourke. 'I made it perfectly clear from the beginning, even in Berlin, that I wanted to stay here for only a few months and then return to Ireland. You accepted this when we first spoke about it here in this flat.'

Stan agreed but pointed out that much had happened since then. Besides endangering the lives of others, he said, the British had a truth drug which they could use on him and which could tell them anything they wanted to know. They had used it on a KGB man in London and afterwards he was sent back to Moscow where he was a physical and mental wreck on pension.

'Don't look so distressed, Seán,' Stan went on. 'I can assure you that you can have a free choice in where to live. Every town in every republic will be open to you. And we will give you every assistance to pursue a worth-while career in publishing.'

Bourke said nothing. Stan got up to leave. 'Good night, Seán,' he said. 'Think about it anyway, and I'll call and see you again in a few days.' Bourke also got up, said good night and shook hands with Stan across the desk. Blake let Stan out of the flat saying unctuously, 'It was nice seeing you,' and proceeded to lock the front door with its double lock. He then went into the study where Bourke was preparing to go to bed.

3

'Well, Robert,' said Blake. 'I understand that you have been having an interesting discussion with Stan.'

'Yes,' Bourke replied coldly. 'I have just been sentenced to five years' imprisonment.'

'I would hardly put it like that.'

'Wouldn't you? Well, that's how I put it.'

'But you've been told you can go anywhere in the Soviet Union.'

'I am told I must stay in a country against my will; that makes me a prisoner. The size of the prison is not relevant.'

'But if you were to return to Ireland,' Blake spoke emphatically, 'you would be handed over to the British and you would finish up in prison anyway.'

'If I were given a free choice,' Bourke replied with equal emphasis, 'I would rather spend the next five years in an English prison on porridge and goulash than spend them here on champagne and caviare.'

'Do you really mean that?'

'Yes, I do. It is a price I would willingly pay for the privilege of living once more among my own people.'

Blake was obviously trying to control his temper, but his face was flushed and he looked angry. 'Tell me,' he asked, 'what exactly don't you like about this country.' To Bourke it seemed a hypocritical question, since he felt, rightly, that Blake also disliked living in the Soviet Union. Bourke's reply was 'Everything'.

'But at least you would be free here,' Blake remarked.
'Free!' Bourke laughed ironically.

You are making a mockery of the word *freedom*. Nobody is free in this bloody country. The Russians don't know what the word means. There is only one mind and one conscience in the Soviet Union, and that's the Communist Party. The people are treated like children. They are told what to think and what to say and what to feel. They read in their so-called 'newspapers' exactly what the Party wants them to read; they hear on Moscow Radio what the Party wants them to hear; and they see on their television screens just what the Party wants them to see. And everybody is afraid to complain. They are frightened and intimidated without fully realizing it, because they have never been otherwise and don't know any different. To the Russian people Lenin is God. For fifty years by command of the Communist Party, the Russian people have prostrated themselves before the image of Lenin in every corner of the land with a fervour and devotion that their forefathers would never have displayed before their icons and their crucifixes. And by God, if the Party decreed tomorrow that Lenin was anti-Communist, these same people would tear down his statues and burn his portraits in the streets!

As he spoke Bourke had worked himself up into quite a rage, which Blake noticed. But Bourke's analysis was apt since this was precisely what happened to Stalin's image as a result of Khrushchev's celebrated speech to the Twentieth Party Congress in 1956.

'Anyway whatever you may think of this country and its people,' Blake said in a quieter tone, 'you yourself could have a comfortable life here. Back home you would be just an ex-convict.'

'I'd rather be digging trenches for the rest of my life in Britain or Ireland,' Bourke retorted, 'than be living in luxury here against my will. And I've had experience of digging trenches.'

Blake went on to remark that the question would not have arisen fifteen years previously, a statement with which Bourke agreed, since he realized that Blake was referring to the terror under Stalin and the then KGB Chief Beria. Finally Blake told Bourke that he was being extremely foolish, after which he left him and went to his room.

Blake spent most of the next day reading *Shadow of a Spy*, the only interruption being a telephone call from Stan to inquire about Bourke. 'Just imagine that!' exclaimed Blake in amazement. 'The KGB ringing up to ask how you feel. Actually concerned about you! Things *have* changed.'

After he had finished reading *Shadow of a Spy*, Blake passed it on to Bourke who read it quite quickly. The author was an Austrian, who wrote under the name of E. H. Cookridge and had been a wartime secret agent, having been imprisoned by the Nazis in two concentration camps. According to Cookridge, Blake had betrayed the Berlin tunnel to the KGB, a great triumph for the Russians, as indeed had been stated at Blake's trial.

'My friend,' replied Blake with a self-satisfied air, 'the KGB knew about the tunnel before the first spadeful of earth was dug out of the ground. I saw to that!'

'Did you?' queried Bourke. 'So all those top secret phone messages that the British and Americans listened in to that year were all specially laid on by the KGB.'

'Naturally,' Blake grinned triumphantly.

A couple of days later, which was Friday, Stan called and went to Blake's room. Bourke, who had put on carpet slippers so that he could not be heard, was in the kitchen, the door of which was as usual ajar. The first question they discussed was Blake's mother, who wished to pay a second visit to her son in December. It was arranged that she should travel overland on the Continent to East Berlin where she would be met by Vladimir and flown to Moscow as before.

Next they spoke about Seán Bourke. 'About our *friend*,' said Blake. 'When you left on Monday I went into his room to talk to him as I told you I would. We had a long discussion about what you had said to him. He completely accepted your decision. There is no doubt about that. He even said he would settle down to learning Russian in earnest. I was quite surprised.'

As Stan said nothing, Blake after a short pause went on: 'Now here's the point. On Wednesday I lent him that book *Shadow of a*

Spy, in which he, of course, is mentioned. Immediately he had finished reading it his whole attitude changed. He said he hated the Soviet Union and wanted to go back to the West. His change of attitude was almost incredible. However, there is no doubt in my mind what his motives are. He doesn't hate the Soviet Union at all. The only reason he wants to go back to the West is so that he can make money out of all this.'

Stan still remained silent, which suggested to Bourke that he was not being very helpful to Blake. 'Of course,' Blake resumed, 'you must remember, Stan, that at the moment the whole world believes that the KGB organized the escape, and that our friend was only used. This means great prestige for your people. Now, if he is allowed to go back to the West and tell his story, your people will no longer get the credit.'

Blake heard Stan get up and pace about the next room, a sure sign that he was worried. At last he spoke. 'I don't think that part of it matters so much,' he said. 'You see, no matter what Seán might write, the public will always believe that we had something to do with the escape. My only concern is for those others who helped.'

'As I see it,' Blake spoke coldly and deliberately, 'you are faced with only two alternatives. You can go out now and tell him that he must stop in the country for at least five years. Or you can . . .'

Blake did not finish the sentence. But it was clear to Bourke what he intended to convey – namely that Bourke should be 'liquidated'.

Bourke went into his own room, dazed by Blake's treachery in trying to make Bourke an enemy of the Soviet Union, although he had never harmed the state or its people in any way. He had a record player and a few records. He chose Beethoven's *Appassionata* played by Richter which he put on. Shortly afterwards Blake came in wearing his red dressing gown and carrying a bottle of champagne and two glasses. 'I say, Robert, what's your attitude to a glass of champagne?' Bourke nodded and took the glass which Blake handed him filled with the bubbling liquid. But the drink tasted bitter.

'Ah', said Blake, 'champagne and beautiful music! What more can one ask for?' Bourke looked at him and could see traces of the scars caused by his fall from the wall of Wormwood Scrubs. Blake's appearance merely served to remind him of his own folly.

Two days later, on Sunday, Bourke invited Blake to lunch at the Ararat, an expensive restaurant near the Bolshoi Theatre, not used as a rule by Intourist for their foreign clientele. Bourke's object was to find out as much as he could about Blake's intention towards himself so that he might be assured that he had not made a mistake. They had roast chicken and a bottle of Georgian red wine. Bourke had made it clear that he intended to pay the bill so that he could order a second bottle. Halfway through the second bottle Bourke raised the subject of Communism.

'Do you think that Communism justifies the use of any means to achieve it?' he asked.

'Most certainly,' replied Blake.

'So I take it then,' said Bourke, 'that you agree with Stalin and Beria?'

Blake looked into his glass. 'Yes,' he said slowly. 'I do agree with them. It may be that innocent people died, but it was worth it. If they hadn't died, there would have been a lot more bloodshed in the long run.' Then, looking at Bourke, he added: 'The end justifies the means.'

Bourke paid the bill and they walked up Marx Prospect until they reached Dzerzhinsky Square, where the Lubyanka and KGB headquarters were located. It was a seven-storey grey building, formerly an insurance office, and now a block with the ground-floor windows barred and screened off above eye level. The square was called after the founder of the Soviet secret police, forerunners of the KGB, Felix Dzerzhinsky, whose life-size statue stood in the middle of the square. At the Metro station opposite, Blake leaned on the railing at the edge of the pavement, looking first at the Lubyanka and then towards the building at right angles to it on the left-hand side of the square. This was a large department store which specialized in children's toys and other children's goods. At the top of the building the words *Detsky Mir* (Children's World) appeared in a large neon sign.

'How very appropriate!' remarked Blake as he looked round.

'Why so?' asked Bourke.

'The KGB offices being next to the Children's World. All this secret service work is so utterly childish,' said Blake. 'One big game.

It makes me laugh. In London we used to call our office the Wimbledon Club.'

'Why was that?'

'Because it was all balls and rackets!'

The only reason why Blake denigrated secret service activities, so it seemed to Seán Bourke, was that he no longer belonged, either to the British or to the Soviet. He had lost his power and the Russians did not have much use for him.

Back in his room in the flat, Bourke pondered about his position. If the second alternative which Blake had posed to Stan was to be carried out, he felt it would be soon. On the other hand, Bourke felt there must be some element of decency in Blake's ruthless makeup, and, surely, Bourke said to himself, Blake must recall that he owed him a favour for what he (Bourke) had done for him in London.

Deciding to beard him, Bourke knocked on Blake's door and went in to his room. Blake was in his red dressing gown and facing the mirror, 'Yes?' he said without turning round.

'I want to return to Ireland,' said Bourke. 'I hope I can count on your support.'

Blake turned round, angered by Bourke's words. 'My support!' he shouted contemptuously. 'Why should *I* give you my support? I don't think you *should* be allowed to leave the Soviet Union. If you want to leave this country that's *your* funeral. Don't come asking *me* for help!'

Bourke turned his back on the man he had so valiantly helped and left the room without a word.

4

Next day, Monday, 4 September 1967, was to be an extremely significant one in the life of Seán Bourke. He left the flat in the early afternoon, telling Blake he was going for a walk. And so he was. But it turned out to be quite a long walk. He began by going up Khmelnitsk Street, crossing the junction with Novaya Square and entering Kuibysheva Street which brought him to Red Square, where the Lenin Mausoleum, St Basil's Cathedral, and the main entrance to the Kremlin are situated. As he traversed the square the Kremlin clock struck four. He then walked across the bridge over the river Moskva, turning right along the Maurice Thorez Embankment towards the British Embassy at No 14. This was, as it still is, a large palatial building constructed in late Tsarist times by a wealthy sugar industrialist called Haritonenko, with a fine view of the Kremlin. There are two gateways to the embassy, one used by cars as an entrance and the other as an exit. As he approached the first gateway, Bourke noticed that the policeman who should have been on guard was at the second gateway talking to the policeman there. With them was an officer in charge. Having satisfied himself by glancing through the first gateway that the embassy was open – in fact it closed at 5 pm – he walked on past the second gateway to the next bridge where he turned and retraced his footsteps. His decision was made to get into the embassy fore-court and defy the KGB.

The two policemen were still talking with the officer when he passed the second gateway. Then, immediately he reached the first one, he turned sharp right and hurried across the forecourt to the embassy entrance. The receptionist showed him into the waiting room and told him he would get someone to see him.

A few minutes later a junior member of the Chancery staff came in and asked Bourke if he could help him.

'Scotland Yard are looking for a man named Seán Bourke in connection with the escape of George Blake from Wormwood Scrubs,' Bourke said.

'Oh, and you know all about it do you?'

'I *am* Seán Bourke.'

'I see,' said the other man. 'Excuse me a moment please.'

'Of course.'

A few minutes later the door opened again and two other men appeared. One was in his late thirties and the other considerably younger.

'I'm Peter Maxey, the embassy First Secretary,' said the older man, 'and this is my colleague.' They shook hands and sat down.

'Well, what exactly is the problem?' Maxey began.

'My name is Bourke, Seán Bourke. Scotland Yard want to see me about the escape of George Blake from prison in London. I've come here to give myself up.'

'And what do you want us to do?' the First Secretary inquired.

'Well,' replied Bourke, who was surprised by the question. 'I was hoping you might be able to help me get back to Britain.'

'Have you got a passport?'

'No.'

'How did you get to this country?'

'With a false passport.'

'Where is the false passport now?'

'The KGB have it.'

'But you're not British are you?'

'No, I'm Irish.'

Mr Maxey looked at his colleague and they both smiled. 'Well,' said the First Secretary, 'how do you expect us to be able to help an Irishman?'

'But it's the British who want to put me on trial,' Bourke protested, 'not the Irish.'

Maxey shrugged and went on with his questions. 'Where is Blake now?'

'He's living here in Moscow and I share his flat.'

'What's the address?'

'I'd rather not say,' Bourke replied. 'It's a KGB flat, and I'm still in Moscow.'

The First Secretary looked thoughtfully at Bourke and said, 'Will you excuse us for a few minutes?'

'Of course,' said Bourke, standing up as they left.

Five minutes later, Maxey returned with another man, aged about forty-five, with grey hair. He was in his shirt sleeves, as if he had hurriedly left his desk.

'This is the Consul,' said Maxey by way of introduction. 'He may be able to help you.'

'Good afternoon, Mr Bourke,' said the Consul. 'I understand that you have no passport.'

'That's right.'

'You are a citizen of the Irish Republic, aren't you?'

'Yes, I am.'

The Consul pushed a writing pad towards him. 'If you would care to write down your full name and date and place of your birth and your address in Ireland,' he said, 'I'll see if I can get you a passport.'

Bourke did as he was requested and handed the paper with his particulars to the Consul, who studied it for a few moments and then said: 'Very well, Mr Bourke, if you care to call back in about a week, I should have something for you.'

Bourke was dumbfounded. 'Call back in a week!' he exclaimed in dismay. 'If I leave this embassy, I shall be dead in twenty-four hours.'

'Well,' the First Secretary intervened, 'you got yourself into this position, didn't you?'

'But what else can we do, Mr Bourke,' the Consul added. 'I shall have to get in touch with our Foreign Office in London and will ask them to approach Dublin, and we shall then have to wait for the Ministry of External Affairs there to forward a passport.'

'But I came here in defiance of the KGB and I rushed in while their backs were turned,' Bourke pleaded. 'Can't you give me asylum?'

'We *can't* give you asylum,' the Consul replied sympathetically. 'You are an Irish citizen and if we tried to make representations to the Russians on your behalf they would just laugh at us and tell us to mind our own business.'

'Is there *any* embassy in Moscow that acts for Ireland?'

'I'm afraid not,' the Consul said, shaking his head. 'Ireland is not represented in any Communist country.'

'Isn't there anywhere at all that I can hide?' Bourke asked in desperation.

'No, Mr Bourke,' said the Consul. 'There's no place for you to hide. Not in *this* country.'

Bourke slowly got to his feet, turned to the window, and pulled back the curtain. The two policemen were standing in their respective gateways, while the Russian officer was standing next to the one on the right; this was the gateway by which Bourke had entered the forecourt. All three were staring at the embassy building. Bourke let go the curtain and turned to the other two.

'Gentlemen,' he said, 'you are unlikely to see me or hear from me again, and I would like to say something which I hope will be passed on to the right quarters. I did, in fact, arrange Blake's escape, and I did it entirely on my own. The KGB were in no way involved. The operation cost only a small sum of money which I was able to borrow from friends.' He added that Blake and he had both travelled on false passports and after they had made contact with the KGB in East Berlin they had both been separately flown to Moscow in a military aircraft. 'I have since been sharing a flat here with Blake, as I have already said,' he continued. 'It was never my intention to stay in the Soviet Union for more than a few months, but now they are reluctant to let me go. As for Blake, it has been said that he was responsible for the deaths of forty-two British agents. Like so many other people I was persuaded by Blake that this was not true. But now I think differently.'

He paused for a few minutes and then went on: 'One night last week I overheard Blake urging the KGB to murder me. Blake is an utterly ruthless man. He is completely devoid of any conscience. Not only does he want me dead, but I now know that he would willingly pull the trigger himself!' The other two looked at him incredulously.

'Well, that's all,' Bourke concluded as he walked towards the door to leave. He noticed the ventilation grille to the right of the door jamb. 'I suppose this place is bugged?'

'Yes,' the First Secretary nodded. 'Well, we assume it is anyway.'

'Just as well,' replied Bourke. 'Perhaps Blake will hear the recording himself. That will be *some* satisfaction.'

Then, after saying good-bye, he made his way to the front door and went down the steps to the forecourt which he crossed to the gateway on the right where the Soviet officer was standing. The officer made no move until Bourke had passed through the gateway to the embankment which was Russian soil. The officer, whom Bourke recognized from the stars on the shoulders of his uniform as a major, blocked the path and said something in Russian. But the only word Bourke could make out was 'passport'.

'*Ya ne poneemaiyoo. Ya Anglisky tourist.*' (I do not understand. I am an English tourist.)

The officer held out his hand again and said, '*Passport.*'

'*Niet,*' said Bourke, pointing in the direction of the Leningradskaya hotel. '*Passport – Leningradskaya gahsteenitse.*' He then took his diary out of his pocket and pointed at the telephone number, saying, '*Telefon! Leningradskaya gahsteenitse.*'

The officer saw the point, namely that foreign tourists had to leave their passports at their hotels. He thought for a minute or two, and to Bourke's surprise finally saluted and walked away. No doubt he realized that it was his fault that Bourke had reached the embassy's British territory initially unobserved.

Bourke walked back to Red Square to hear the Kremlin clock strike six. It was an hour since he had left the embassy and the KGB who must now have known about his visit, would probably send someone to Red Square thinking he might well be there. So Bourke hurried on, passing the Bolshoi Theatre and up Pushkin Street to the Boulevard. There was a Journalistic Club nearby which he entered, expecting he might get a drink from a friendly British or American journalist, but everyone he saw in the foyer was Russian and eventually he was turned away because he had no pass. He walked on along the Boulevard until he reached Arbat Square, where he looked at his watch. It was 7.30. Outside the Arbat Metro station there was a telephone kiosk. Bourke went in, lifted the receiver, inserted a 2-kopek piece, and dialled the number of the flat. Blake answered.

'Hello! This is Seán here. Now listen carefully. I have something very important to tell you. I have just been to the British Embassy and asked them to help me get back to Ireland.'

'You have done *what*?' Blake shouted.

'I have been to the British Embassy.'

'You fool! You complete and utter fool! What did you do that for?'

'Because I'm sick and tired of you and the KGB and this cloak-and-dagger life,' Bourke shouted back. 'I'm sick and tired of being a pawn in your little game of revenge against the British secret service. I'm sick of the whole bloody business. I want to return to a normal life. I want to go back to Ireland on an Irish passport made out in my own name and I want to be myself again.'

'And how do you think you are going to do that?' The sarcastic tone of Blake's voice was unmistakable.

'The British have asked me to call back in a week to collect my Irish passport,' Bourke answered. 'I shall then go to the Soviet Foreign Ministry and apply for an exit visa. From now on it's going to be all aboveboard.'

'And do you think you are going to get away with that!'

'I'm going to try.' But Bourke realized that Blake was right. Every Western embassy in Moscow would now be closely guarded by the KGB as would the Foreign Ministry. Bourke would not get near the British Embassy.

'You are even more stupid than I thought you were,' said Blake with his customary contempt. 'And that's really saying something.'

'You may think so,' said Bourke, 'but I don't agree.'

'You never told *me* you were going to do this, did you?' Blake went on to ask. The question was not as stupid as it sounded, since Blake's telephone, like every other telephone in a KGB 'safe house', was carefully monitored, and Blake wanted the KGB to hear Bourke exonerate him. Bourke appreciated this.

'Why *should* I tell you? Why should I tell you anything?'

'You *are* stupid,' Blake shouted again. 'You really are stupid. You are a stupid fool!'

'I can't understand you,' Bourke shouted back. 'I can't understand you at all – *comrade*! Any other man in your position would be shouting at the top of his voice, "Let him go, let him go! If the man wants to go home, for God's sake let him go! He has done me a great favour and he is at least entitled to that much!" But not you, oh no, not you. I just can't understand you.'

'How dare you talk to me like that?' Blake screamed. 'How dare you? What gives you the right to say things like that to me?'

Bourke said nothing, feeling as he did that Blake was mentally unbalanced and only a madman could betray him and then ask him how he dared object.

After a prolonged pause, Blake spoke again, this time more calmly. 'And what are you going to do now?'

'I'm just going to wander through the streets for the next week and then go back to the British Embassy for my passport.'

'But you can't do that. The police will pick you up.'

'I'll get by.'

'But why not come back and wait here, and you can still go to the embassy in a week's time?'

'I'd rather not,' said Bourke who realized that Blake was deliberately stalling to give the KGB time to trace the call. 'I want to be alone with my thoughts.'

'I see,' said Bourke. 'And where are you calling from?'

'A phone-box somewhere in Moscow.' With that Bourke hung up and left the kiosk.

5

Bourke went into the Arbat Metro station and took the first train which came along and which happened to be going west, although he had no idea of the direction until the train stopped at the next station Smolenskaya, where some people got in as they did at the succeeding two stations, after which more people left. Bourke sat on until the train reached Molodyoznaha which was the end of the line, and where he followed the few remaining passengers up the escalator to the street. He found himself in a residential suburb at the western edge of the city. Here he realized that Blake was right and that he could not wander through the streets for a week, as a policeman could ask to see his papers and he had none. By this time it was eight o'clock and it was beginning to get dark. He remembered that there was a public park at Ismailova at the opposite end of the city. Unwilling to make the journey by Metro which would take him through the centre of Moscow, he saw a taxi and asked the driver in Russian to drive him to the station there. The journey, in which Bourke sat beside the driver in Soviet style, took half an hour and the fare was 2 roubles 70 kopeks. Bourke gave the driver 4 roubles, which left him with only 5 roubles in his wallet, the equivalent of £2.

The Ismailova, an estate of some 3,000 acres, much of it forest, formerly belonged to the Romanovs and was a favourite retreat of the Tsars and their families in the summer. It was now growing dark. But Bourke went into the forest where his eyes soon became used to the darkness and he was able to avoid colliding with trees. Presently he found a clearing where he made a bed of leaves from a birch tree. He lay down on this improvised bed but made no attempt to sleep, since he felt cold and he was wearing a thin summer suit and had no coat since it was quite sunny and warm when he left the flat. Every half hour through the night he got up and did five minutes' exercises in an endeavour to keep warm. With the approach of dawn he walked back to the park where he encountered some early risers picking mushrooms. He pretended to be on the same errand keeping his eyes looking to the ground.

By this time he felt hungry, so he went into a food shop at the entrance to the park where he bought a kilogram of salami and a bottle of milk, also a copy of *Pravda* and other papers to sit on when he returned to the damp forest. There he walked about for the rest of the morning. In the afternoon he decided to phone the flat to relieve his boredom and see if Blake might give some information about what the KGB were doing in relation to himself.

First, he boarded a tram going south but well away from the city centre. After half an hour he got off and went into a telephone kiosk where he dialled the number of the flat. Blake answered.

'Hello,' said Bourke. 'This is Seán here.'

'Oh, hello Seán. How are you?' It was the first time Blake had called him Seán since he had moved into the flat. Where was he sleeping? And what was he doing for food? Bourke guessed that Blake's purpose was to keep him talking until the KGB had traced the call and reached the place where he was speaking from.

'There's no need to be worried,' said Bourke. 'I can look after myself.'

'I do wish you'd come back, Seán. I really do.'

Bourke's reply showed he was no fool. 'I know as well as you do that this phone is tapped and at this moment a car is on its way here. So I'll say good-bye.'

'Well, will you call again Seán?'

'Yes, I'll call tomorrow.'

With that Bourke hung up and jumped on the first tram he saw heading north. He got out at the newspaper stall beside the entrance to Ismailova Park and bought some more papers and several magazines, after which he went across the park into the forest. There he had another sleepless night, and regularly got up to do his exercises, using the magazines to lie on and the papers to cover himself in a further attempt to keep warm. Again he met the mushroom gatherers at dawn and bought some salami and milk. This left him with just a rouble and he had to decide whether to go back to the forest and die of cold or give himself up to the KGB regardless of any punishment he might receive from that source.

In the afternoon he took the Metro going west from the station at Ismailova Park and got out four stops later at Kursk, the nearest to the block of flats where Blake lived. There was a telephone kiosk at the end of the lane leading to the flats. Bourke went in and dialled Blake's number. The following dialogue ensued after Blake answered the call.

'Hello, Seán here.'

'Hello, Seán, how are you?'

'Fine.'

'Seán, I'm worried about you. You're getting nothing to eat, are you?'

'I'm not doing too badly.'

'But the nights are getting so cold. You can't go on like this.'

'Why can't I?'

'Well, you'll catch a cold, you'll get ill.'

'I've got great stamina.'

'That may be so, but no one can survive these conditions for very long. It really is very foolish.'

'I'll manage,' said Bourke. He thought how things had changed since he had spoken to Blake that first night by walkie-talkie.

'Look, Seán,' Blake pleaded, 'why don't you come back here? You can't go running round for ever. Why not come back now?'

Bourke pondered over this question for a few moments, conclud-
ing that all things considered he might as well. So he told Blake.

'You will. You'll come?'

'Yes.'

'Oh, good,' said Blake. 'Good boy. That's very sensible.' He
sounded genuinely relieved, as indeed he was.

'I'll be there in half an hour.'

In fact, it only took three minutes to reach the flat from where
Bourke was speaking. But he had a good reason for saying what he
did. He walked along the lane, went into the block by the front
door and climbed the stairs to the flat where he stopped and put his
ear to the keyhole. He could hear Blake dialling a number. 'Hallo,
Stan,' Blake said. 'He's coming in . . . Yes. He's on his way now.
He should be here in about twenty minutes or so . . . Yes, I suggest
you send someone along to make sure he isn't being followed . . .
You will? Good . . . Very well, Stan, I'll call you when he arrives.
Good-bye.'

Bourke walked round the block for about five minutes and then
returned to the flat and rang the bell. Blake opened the door. 'Well,
you're back,' he said, smiling. 'You're early.'

'I caught a bus.'

'Come in, come in. My, you look rough.' Sure enough, Bourke
had a two days' growth of beard, a crumpled, dirty suit and muddy
shoes. 'You'd better have a bath while I cook you something.'

The dining-room door opened and Victor came into the hall.
'Victor has been sleeping here for the past couple of nights,' Blake
explained. 'We weren't sure what had happened to you, or whose
hands you had fallen into, so they sent Victor along shortly after
you phoned the first time.'

Victor was wearing a dark suit and Bourke noticed an ominous
bulge under his left arm, but Bourke gave no sign that he realized
that Victor was carrying a weapon. All he said was, 'I could do with
that bath, so if you'll excuse me . . .'

While Bourke was in the bath, Blake cooked an excellent meal,
with four rashers of bacon, two eggs, fried tomatoes, a pot of tea
and bread and butter. Blake served the meal with a smile, at the
same time good-humouredly plying Bourke with questions. Whom

did he meet at the British Embassy? Where had he been sleeping, and so on. Bourke told Blake everything he wanted the KGB to know, while Victor stood silently in the background. When the meal was finished Blake suggested that Bourke should try to get some sleep. 'You look like you need it.'

Bourke went into the study and made up his bed. He then opened the desk drawer and found all his photographs missing as well as the manuscript of the escape story he had written, dealing mainly with his life in Wormwood Scrubs. Before going to sleep he heard Blake dialling the telephone. 'Hello, Stan! He's here . . . Yes, he arrived about three-quarters of an hour ago. He's gone to bed now . . . All right I'll call you later in the evening.'

Stan arrived in a couple of hours. Bourke got up, dressed, put the couch back in its place in the wall, moving about to let the others know he was awake. They came in shortly afterwards. 'Hello, Seán,' said Stan, and to Bourke's surprise held out his hand, which Bourke took and shook. Victor then left, and Blake came back into the study after he had showed him out.

'Well,' said Bourke, 'when does the inquest begin?'

'There's no question of an inquest,' Stan replied in quite a friendly manner. 'I'd just like to have a chat with you. I hope we can talk frankly to each other like friends.'

'Well,' said Bourke, 'as you will know by now, I dodged past the policemen to get into the British Embassy. I asked them to get me a passport so that I can go home in a perfectly legal manner and return to a normal way of life. They took my particulars and said they would do what I asked and that I should call back in a week.'

'But there was no need for you to do that, Seán,' said Stan quietly.

'I think there was, Stan. It's my future and happiness that's at stake, and no one else's . . . When I came to Moscow, you agreed that I should stay here for only a few months. And then last Friday you told me that I would have to stay here for at least five years.'

Stan looked hurt. 'But Seán, I only meant you to *consider* the proposal. I asked you to think it over. If you were in such a hurry to go home, you should have told me and I would have arranged it for you.'

'Stan, I considered, and still consider, that in the long run this is the best way out for everyone. I am relieving everyone of a great deal of inconvenience. Now you don't have to go to the trouble of issuing me with false travel documents and all the rest of it. This is much simpler. I go back to Ireland and fight extradition.'

'Very well, Seán, if that's how you want it,' said Stan. 'The decision is yours.' He paused for a few moments and then went on: 'By the way, would you mind having a look at some photographs and see if you can recognize the diplomats who spoke to you? But you needn't do it if you don't like.'

'I have no objections at all.'

Stan then took a long envelope out of his pocket and handed it to Bourke. It contained about a dozen postcard-size photographs, the subjects being formally posed, the inference being that they were enlarged passport photographs. At the bottom of each picture was a name spelt phonetically in letters of the Russian alphabet. Bourke had no difficulty in picking out the four diplomats whom he had talked to as well as the receptionist inside the front door to whom he had spoken first.

'Do you think any of them were in British secret intelligence?' Stan asked.

'I wouldn't be at all surprised.'

Asked how he had been treated, Bourke answered that with the exception of the Consul they seemed rather pleased that he was in trouble.

'I see,' said Stan, putting the photographs back in his pocket. 'And did they find out your address?'

'Mr Maxey, the First Secretary did ask for it, but all I told him was that I was sharing a flat with George Blake somewhere in Moscow.'

'Anyway,' said Stan, sounding relieved, 'I'm glad you didn't give them the address.' Asked what his plans were, Bourke repeated that he wished to go back to Ireland.

'Very well, Seán. I'll make the necessary arrangements. I don't think it would be a good idea for you to get your passport through the British. This would enable them to know too much about your plans, and they might try to intercept you on the way. I think we should try some other channel. Will you leave it in my hands?'

'Yes, of course, whatever you say.' Bourke could hardly believe his good fortune since he had expected to be arrested on his return to the flat and taken to the Lubyanka, perhaps to be executed. He glanced at Blake who looked bewildered and angry, while saying nothing.

'And are you in a *desperate* hurry?' Stan went on to ask Bourke. 'Or can you wait for a few months?'

'Well, now that I know I'm leaving and that you are going to make the arrangements, I suppose another few months won't make any difference.'

'I'm glad you see it that way, Seán. I think it would be in your own interests to let things cool off a little before making the move.'

Stan leaned back thoughtfully and looked at Blake and then at Bourke before telling them what he had in mind. 'Well, now, gentlemen, the position seems to be this. Until last Monday the British did not know that you were both here. Your letters from Cairo and London confused them. But now that they do know, they are going to be looking for you. There is a real danger that MI6 and even the CIA will try to get you. I suggest, therefore, that you should leave Moscow for a while. I shall arrange a tour of the Soviet Union for you. You'll enjoy the tour anyway so it will be mixing business with pleasure. You can stay away at least a month.'

Blake and Bourke each said this sounded interesting. 'Yes, it should be,' Stan nodded. 'You can start with the Baltic states and work your way east as far as Tashkent.'

'When do we start?'

'Perhaps in a week. I'll have to make a lot of arrangements. In the meantime we shall have to give you a bodyguard for your own protection while you're waiting for the tour to begin. We can't take any chances with the other side.' Then, looking at Bourke, Stan added: 'By the way, Seán, please don't go to the British Embassy again, for *my* sake. If you do, you will be causing a great deal of trouble for me personally.' Bourke promised he wouldn't.

'Robert, you're a very lucky man,' said Blake after Stan had left. 'You took a great risk in going to the British Embassy. You're lucky you weren't shot. You gambled with your life and you won. The KGB think you are a very brave man. They told me so.'

'Brave – bollocks!' said Bourke. 'For me the choice was very simple. I would *rather* be dead than spend the rest of my life in the Soviet Union. It had nothing to do with bravery.'

The bodyguard consisted of six men and two girls and they were installed in a house overlooking the entrance to the block of flats. They worked in shifts, two men and a girl to a shift, and they were no inconvenience, following at a discreet distance when Blake and Bourke went out for a walk and going by car if Blake and Bourke took a bus. To make their task easier, Blake and Bourke each told them in advance where they were going, singly or together.

A week passed, but there was no sign of the tour starting. Then something happened in London which forced the KGB's hand, since the Prime Minister Harold Wilson was personally involved. The incident concerned Dr Vladimir Kachenko, a twenty-five-year-old Soviet physicist researching low temperature physics at Birmingham University, one of the ninety Soviet scientists working in London at the time.

At 4.40 am on Saturday 16 September, Kachenko turned up at the Soviet Embassy in Kensington Palace Gardens and rang the bell. The night doorman who answered it told the young scientist to come back at nine o'clock in the morning which he did. Two and a half hours later Kachenko left the embassy and walked up Kensington Palace Gardens, turning right at the end to Bayswater Road and Lancaster Gate. There he was spotted by someone in an MI5 observation post. At the same time a Soviet Embassy car, which had been following Kachenko, stopped beside him and he was bundled into the vehicle before anyone could intervene. An hour or so later a group of Soviet diplomats ushered the apparently dazed scientist aboard an Aeroflot Tupolev 204 at Heathrow bound for Moscow. The aircraft then began to move away from the departure gate, and was preparing for take off when the pilot was ordered by the traffic controllers to stop. The machine was then surrounded by police cars, and Kachenko, who appeared barely conscious, was removed and driven in an ambulance to an MI5 apartment. Here he was seen by an eminent psychiatrist who diagnosed acute schizophrenia. Because he had received an injection, presumably at the Soviet Embassy, the psychiatrist advised that, since the drug he had

had was unknown and it was not possible to give him the requisite antidote and his condition was deteriorating, he should be returned to the embassy. This was done on the Monday morning and there he was joined by his wife Galina who called a press conference at which she accused the British of trying to kidnap her husband and said she had written to the Prime Minister. After consulting the MI5 chief, Sir Martin Furnival Jones, Mr Wilson rejected Mrs Kachenko's charge that the police had behaved improperly. 'It appeared to the police that your husband was being put aboard the plane against his will,' Mr Wilson replied to Mrs Kachenko. 'If, as you say, this was a mistaken impression resulting from the fact that your husband was ill, then the proper course would have been for the authorities at the Soviet Embassy to ask for our help with the problem.' In fact the scientist wished to go to Moscow and in the event he and his wife were flown there the next day.

Whilst these diplomatic manœuverings were taking place, Stan telephoned Blake and spoke to him at length. Questioned afterwards by Bourke, Blake said: 'It seems that MI6 were trying to recruit him. They thought they had won him over, but the KGB were also trying to use him. In the end Kachenko was heading for a nervous breakdown so the KGB decided to get him back to Moscow.'

By way of retaliation, on Wednesday 20 September, the Foreign Office released the news of Bourke's visit to the British Embassy in Moscow. Bourke first heard the news on the BBC World Service, and was relieved that there was no mention of his denunciation of Blake. It was stated simply that Bourke had gone to the embassy to ask for help in getting home and had been told to call back in a few days but had failed to do so.

Stan called at the flat that night and confirmed that the Foreign Office statement had been broadcast for the purpose of drawing attention away from the Kachenko incident. 'We also believe,' Stan went on, 'that if Kachenko had agreed to stay in Britain, the British secret service would have quietly offered to hand him back to us in return for you, Seán!'

Stan added that no less than ten foreign correspondents had called at the British Embassy that day and had filed stories suggesting among other things that Seán Bourke was in trouble.

'Anyway,' Stan concluded, looking at both men, 'this now means that you must both definitely leave Moscow within the next couple of days.'

6

On 23 September 1967, Blake and Bourke caught the overnight Moscow–Leningrad express (The Red Arrow) with a comfortable sleeping car. They were accompanied by a KGB Major Vladislava Komarov, known for short as Slava. At the Oktyabrskaya station in Leningrad they were met by another KGB officer with a car and were accommodated in the hotel of the same name on the Ligovsky Prospect opposite the station. This was not the type of first-class hotel used by Intourist for foreign visitors but was quite adequate in the circumstances. In addition to the car, two guides were supplied, the reason being that Blake wished to visit the Hermitage and other art galleries and palaces, while Bourke opted for breweries and champagne plants. However, during their week in Leningrad, they both went to the ballet, seeing *Swan Lake* and *Spartacus*, where they sat in the old imperial box, which had been reserved for them by the local office of the KGB. Their hosts at factories and the like were invariably told that they were 'important officials from England visiting the Soviet Union as guests of the Soviet Union'.

Bourke's guide was a twenty-five-year-old brunette called Valentina. One day she took Bourke on a trip to the Gulf of Finland, where there were several resorts and spas, also no doubt a champagne plant, besides the old imperial palaces of Peterhof and Gatchina. After spending half-an-hour gazing across the gulf, they returned to Leningrad, and Valentina, with whom Bourke had become friendly, indeed more than friendly, suggested that he might like to see her flat. He said he would and stayed there the night. There was a telephone in the flat and Bourke called Slava at the Oktyabrskaya Hotel to tell him that he would not be coming back for the night, knowing that he would be in trouble if he had not telephoned. 'Well,' said Blake next day when he learned of Bourke's nocturnal adventure, 'that puts you one up on me, Robert!'

Throughout the tour they were treated as VIPs and everywhere wined and dined by the local KGB. From Leningrad they went by train to Vilnius, the capital of Lithuania, where they spent four days. On one of the days they drove to a health resort in a forest, lunching on their way at Kaunas, the temporary Lithuanian capital between the two World Wars. At Kaunas they drank a lot of brandy and at a café further along the road still more brandy. These libations loosened their tongues, and Slava brought up the question of Bourke's controversial visit to the British Embassy. 'I must say, Seán, I was very disappointed with you doing a thing like that,' said Slava. 'Very disappointed indeed.'

'Naturally, you're disappointed,' Bourke replied. 'But as I saw it, I was acting in my own interests. If there had been an Irish Embassy in Moscow I would have gone there, but there wasn't. I don't see any reason why I should apologize for what I did. I am an Irish citizen who wants to go back to Ireland.'

'That's all right,' Slava agreed. 'But the way you went about it was very unprofessional. You could never work for our organization. Never!'

'Thanks be to God for that,' Bourke retorted, making an elaborate sign of the cross.

Blake turned towards Bourke. 'The trouble with you is that you are so selfish,' he sneered. 'You are thinking only of yourself. Those other people in London will be put in danger if you go back to Ireland, but that doesn't seem to worry you.'

'If anybody around here is selfish, it is you,' Bourke replied. 'You are thinking only of yourself. You are no more concerned about those people in London than you are about me, except that you wouldn't want them to be arrested so that you could have the last laugh on the British. That's why you don't want to leave the Soviet Union – because if I were extradited the British secret service would be one up on you. So don't try and kid me!'

'Do you *want* to give the British the last laugh? Do you like them? Look at the trick they played on me. Forty-two years!'

'Yes, it was a long sentence,' Bourke agreed. 'But you weren't exactly nicked for shoplifting!'

'And you like them for that, do you?' Blake persisted.

Bourke reminded Blake that if it were not for the freedom-loving English and the English way of life, they would not have been able to do what they did at Wormwood Scrubs. Blake pooh-poohed this remark as 'rubbish'.

'I am free today because of your bravery and the bravery of the other people who helped us,' said Blake, who hoped to impress their KGB companions.

'Bravery – bollocks!' Bourke retorted contemptuously. 'Bravery, like everything else, is relative . . . There was no bravery needed to throw a rope ladder over an unguarded prison wall in London. You are a lucky man that the situation wasn't reversed and that you weren't doing your sentence in a Soviet prison, because then you would never have escaped. And you would have been wasting your time asking anyone to spring you. That would really require *courage*.'

'Nonsense,' remarked Blake in astonishment.

'I'll believe that,' Bourke said, 'when I see Soviet students demonstrating in Red Square in protest against writers and other dissidents being sent to labour camps in Siberia or the Arctic Circle.'

'You know, for someone who has had all the help you have had in this country,' said Blake, 'you are not very grateful. You are here in this country and enjoying this country's hospitality on *my* say-so. Do you realize that?'

'It is no use you pretending to be concerned about me or pretending to admire my "bravery", because I happen to know that you have nothing but the utmost contempt for me,' Bourke rejoined. 'I once heard you say to Stan, who is a KGB officer, that I was "just an Irish peasant" who didn't know what he wanted.'

Blake looked embarrassed and confused. 'W-w-well,' he began hesitantly, 'when I used the word *peasant* I was naturally referring to your love of your own country and your attachment to that land. That is all I meant.' Nevertheless, Blake's explanation did not sound very convincing, although Slava tried to cover up for him by saying that there was nothing wrong with being a peasant, like their Lithuanian guide whose parents were peasants on a collective farm.

[137]

However, for the first time Bourke had succeeded in putting Blake on the defensive.

Bourke went on to refer to the night when he was making a cup of tea in the kitchen of Blake's flat, when he overheard Blake telling Stan that in his opinion there were only two alternative ways of dealing with him: 'You can go out and tell him he has got to stay in this country whether he likes it or not – or . . .'

Blake lowered his eyes looking at the floor, and asked: 'Did you hear the second alternative?'

'No,' Bourke lied. 'The kettle boiled just then and so I made the tea and went back to my room.'

'I see,' said Blake, now thoroughly embarrassed.

'I think you are an extremely ruthless man,' Bourke went on emphatically.

Blake now looked ashamed as well as embarrassed, his sense of shame due to the impression he had given Slava and the others in the car that he stood out as a man who would betray someone who had helped him. There was an awkward silence and no one spoke for the rest of the journey.

They all spent the night at the health resort and returned to Vilnius next day. On the following morning, Blake, Bourke and Slava flew to Odessa, where much to Bourke's delight their first excursion was to a champagne plant where they were hospitably entertained by the manager, who gave Bourke a bottle to take away. For some drinkers Russian champagne is too sweet compared with the usual dry French brands, but Bourke always enjoyed it, as did Blake, and they both imbibed the bubbling liquid freely.

In their hotel Blake and Bourke had adjacent rooms, while Slava's room was at the end of the corridor. They parted, when Bourke excused himself to go to the lavatory. When he emerged he put his key in the lock of the bedroom door but could not open it. 'What's the matter with this bloody lock?' he muttered audibly.

At this moment four smartly dressed young Indians appeared and started to let themselves into the two opposite rooms. 'Excuse me, you speak English?' asked one of the Indians who heard Bourke's muttered words when he was trying to open his door.

'Yes, I do,' replied Bourke. 'I speak English for the same reason you gentlemen do. Your country and mine have one thing in common: we both kicked out the English.'

'Oh, where are you from then?' asked one of the Indians.

'I am an Irishman,' said Bourke. 'I come from the city of Limerick and my street is called after one of your provinces – Bengal Terrace.'

All the Indians smiled and shook hands. 'And what are you gentlemen doing in Odessa?' Bourke asked them.

'We're in the Indian Merchant Navy,' the first one explained. 'We are trainee officers and our ship is being fumigated in the harbour at the moment and that's why we have to stay in a hotel. And you?'

'Oh, well, I'm . . . let's say . . . a tourist.'

In the course of the brief conversation which followed, the fact of hotel rooms in the Soviet Union being bugged was mentioned.

'They're all supposed to be bugged?' one of the Indians asked.

'From what I read in the papers, it would appear some of them are,' Bourke replied. 'I remember reading some time ago about an English MP that the Russians didn't like; they planted a bird on him in his Moscow hotel and photographed them in bed together. The MP lost his wife and his parliamentary seat.'[1]

Slava then emerged from his room at the end of the corridor and walked towards them. 'I suggest we talk about India because the man coming this way is a policeman,' Bourke spoke in a low voice.

'Hello, Seán,' said Slava frowning. Bourke thereupon introduced him to the Indians, telling him why they were in the hotel, and going on to talk with the Indians and Slava about India's economic problems.

When it became clear to Bourke that Slava was not going to leave him alone with the Indians, Bourke excused himself and this time succeeded in opening the door of his room. He went in followed by Slava and Blake who had come out of his room next door. 'Seán,'

---

[1] The MP was Commander Anthony Courtney, a Conservative who represented East Harrow. The incident took place at the National Hotel in Moscow in 1961, the lady being an Intourist guide presumably also working for the KGB. Courtney was unmarried at the time, but his wife Lady Trefgarne, whom he married in 1962, divorced him after he lost the seat to Labour at the 1966 General Election. See his *Sailor in a Russian Frame* (1968) for a full account of the affair.

Slava spoke with annoyance, 'I thought we agreed before this tour started that we would avoid contact with foreigners.'

'We did,' Bourke agreed. 'But those men spoke to me first. What did you expect me to do – ignore them?'

'You needn't have ignored them, but at the same time you didn't have to spend a quarter of an hour talking to them. They might have recognized you.'

'I doubt it.'

'Well,' said Slava, 'they were all very quiet when I appeared. Did you tell them who I was?'

'No, I didn't,' lied Bourke.

'Well, I wish you would consider *our* problem,' Slava went on. 'We are trying to keep you away so that you will not be recognized and so that our Foreign Office won't be embarrassed any more. That is the whole point of this tour.'

'I don't mean *that* much to the Soviet Foreign Office or to the KGB,' said Bourke, snapping his fingers. 'Nothing could be more convenient for your people than that I should drop dead at this moment.'

'If you think that's their attitude to you,' Blake intervened, 'why haven't they just destroyed you?'

'And am I supposed to feel grateful for not being shot?' Bourke queried.

'What is all this about being shot?' asked Slava, sounding shocked.

'Don't ask me,' said Bourke, pointing at Blake, 'ask him. When he says destroy, he means plain murder.'

'What is all this nonsense about shooting and murder?' asked Slava. 'Do you think we do things like that?'

'Oh, for Christ's sake, Slava, don't take me for a bloody fool!'

'What do you mean?'

'What do I mean? Haven't you heard of Beria?'

Slava said nothing, but looked embarrassed.

'Yes, Beria,' Bourke continued. 'The mass murderer. I'm sure you've heard of him. Some of your braver modern poets have certainly heard of him. He's the psychopathic killer who shot all those innocent people on Stalin's orders. So don't look so shocked and incredulous!'

Slava blushed red, as Bourke had never seen him do before, 'Stalin was a great war leader,' was all he would say.

'Stalin was a cold-blooded murderer,' Bourke exclaimed.

'If you think we are so wicked, why haven't *you* been harmed?' Slava asked quietly.

'Because, Slava,' replied Bourke, 'I believe that you and Stan and your other comrades in Dzerzhinsky Square are decent, honourable men sincerely searching for an amicable solution to this problem.'

Slava looked relieved. 'Thank you, Seán,' he said, adding, as he left the room, 'I would ask you to try to keep away from foreigners for the remainder of the tour – as a favour to me.'

'All right, Slava, I'll do that,' said Bourke, who then said good-night to the others and went to bed.

Next day they all went to have lunch in a fishing village about twenty miles along the coast from Odessa. Afterwards they drove back to their hotel, a different one from that they had been in before, since it was clear that Slava was determined that Bourke should not meet the Indians again.

From Odessa they flew to Sochi, where they were met at the airport by Bourke's old friend Valodya who gave them a warm welcome since he now knew who Bourke really was besides recalling his amorous adventures during his previous visit. After a week's sunbathing on the Sochi beaches they flew on to Yerevan, the picturesque Armenian capital. There they naturally called at the KGB office for any mail which Blake was expecting and which Stan had promised to forward from Moscow.

There were two letters for Blake, one from his mother and the other from one of his sisters. He ripped open the latter first. 'Well, that's all right,' he said smiling as he read his sister's. 'My sister is in good spirits.' He opened the other envelope and began to read his mother's letter. Suddenly his smile vanished and he was silent and glum. He put both envelopes in his pocket and said nothing for twenty minutes while they were waiting for Slava. Instinctively Bourke felt that Mrs Blake had learned through the Foreign Office in London that Blake had urged the KGB to kill him.

After attending a concert that night they returned to their hotel, where, owing to the presence of an official conference in Yerevan, there was a great demand for hotel accommodation and Bourke had to share a room with Slava, while Blake had a room to himself. As they were preparing to go to bed, Slava asked to be excused and left the room. After a few minutes Bourke followed along the carpeted corridor to Blake's room, raising his hand as if he was about to knock in case anyone else passed the door but really cupping his hand to his ear and listening through the keyhole.

Blake was talking and sounded agitated. 'But that's exactly what it says, Slava, I've just told you.'

'You are sure there cannot be a misunderstanding?' Slava asked.

'Of course I'm sure. It's perfectly plain language.'

'And it is in Dutch?'

'Yes, my mother and I always write to each other in Dutch. Look, Slava, Stan must know about this immediately. I'll translate it tonight and give it to you first thing in the morning and you can phone it to Moscow.'

'Very well, George. You haven't mentioned this to Seán, have you?'

'No, of course not. He mustn't be told.'

Bourke returned to his room followed by Slava a few minutes later. They said little before turning out the light. But next morning, while Bourke pretended to be asleep, there was a knock on the door. Slava got up and opened the door to find Blake who said audibly, 'This is the translation for you, Slava.' Slava replied that he would send it off after breakfast, which presumably he did since he was away in the KGB office for some time.

At first Blake wished to return to Moscow immediately, since, as he told Slava, he did not want to continue the tour with Bourke after reading his mother's letter. But Slava dissuaded him and so the tour continued, including a celebration dinner on 28 October, the anniversary of Blake's escape from Wormwood Scrubs, Blake going so far as to propose a toast 'To Robert'.

From Yerevan they flew to Tashkent and Bukhara, back to Tashkent and then on to Krasnovodsk on the evening of 15 November. Stan was waiting for them with a car at Kursk station and drove them to Blake's flat nearby, while Slava caught a taxi home.

7

Stan was his usual courteous self and had even taken the trouble to bring some food along with him in case the fridge was empty. While he was talking to Blake in the dining room, Bourke prepared a light meal in the kitchen. Bourke heard the other two talking in low tones and was sure Blake was telling Stan more about what his mother had written in her letter. When the meal was ready Stan joined them, but gave no sign of what he had heard from Blake. He was solely interested in the tour, which had lasted just short of two months, and asked for full details. He only mentioned one thing which had happened in Moscow during their absence. Seán Bourke's brother Kevin had phoned the British Embassy to inquire about him. 'And while he was talking, Seán,' Stan added, 'there was a woman's voice in the background.'

'Probably his wife,' said Seán, though he knew it was much more likely to be the voice of the English monitor taping their conversation for MI5.

A few days later Stan again visited the flat, this time bringing with him a bunch of English newspapers, including those of 22 September and subsequent dates giving particulars of Seán Bourke's visit to the Moscow Embassy. The story figured prominently and was illustrated by photographs of Bourke and Blake. There was also a hint that Bourke might have got into trouble with his Soviet hosts since a member of the embassy staff had reported seeing him being stopped by the police officer at the gateway as he left.

'I'm afraid, Seán, that I have some bad news for you,' said Stan, handing Bourke some of the papers. 'Your mother is dead. She died in March but we only discovered it by reading these papers. I'm very sorry, Seán.'

'That's all right, Stan,' Bourke replied. 'She was seventy-five and had a peaceful, healthy life.'

Shortly afterwards during a visit to the circus with Slava, Bourke learned of Mrs Blake's forthcoming visit to Moscow to stay with her son. Slava thought it would not be a good idea for Bourke to meet her, since she was bound to report the meeting when she returned home, which would cause complications. This was confirmed by Stan when he and Bourke met for dinner at the Metropole Hotel a few days later. 'We're trying to get the British to think you have left this country and gone somewhere else,' said Stan. 'We mustn't provoke the British by flaunting you in front of people because they then might be tempted to make a formal application to our Foreign Ministry to have you handed over. I have checked on this and have been assured that you will not be handed over in any circumstances; but still we mustn't be provocative.'

'That sounds reasonable enough,' was Bourke's comment. 'But how are the British going to be convinced that I have left the Soviet Union?'

'We have dropped little hints here and there,' Stan answered. 'Also I think it would be a good idea if you would write a letter to someone in your family and we will have it posted somewhere else, perhaps in Austria.'

As a result of this conversation, Bourke wrote to his twin brother Kevin in Scotland. He also wrote to Yuri Andropov, the KGB chief in Dzerzhinsky Square, thanking him for the generous hospitality he had received in the Soviet Union and pointing out that his stay had only been intended to be a short one and that he would never be content until he had once more set foot on Irish soil. Stan was surprised by this second letter in English, a language in which Andropov was fluent, and agreed to pass it on, which no doubt he did.

The original idea was that Bourke should be moved to another flat during Mrs Blake's stay, but the flat was not ready so that Slava took him and his luggage to the Warsaw Hotel, where he was installed in Room 207 in the name of Komarov. At the same time Slava told him that he was arranging for him to have someone in the way of a guide while he was staying in the hotel. A friend who was a lecturer at Moscow University had arranged to supply a young girl student who was studying languages including English and would welcome an opportunity of meeting someone from Britain on whom she could practise her English. 'I am meeting this girl tomorrow and I'll bring her along to see you.' Slava added, 'Oh, and by the way, I am from Intourist.'

'I understand.'

'One final point, Seán,' said Slava. 'Be sure to avoid restaurants like the National and the other places we have told you about, especially when you are with George. We know for a fact that the Americans at one time planned to shoot Donald Maclean in a Moscow restaurant.[1] Don't tell George – it might upset him.'

The following afternoon there was a knock on the door of Room 207 in the Warsaw Hotel. 'Come in,' Bourke called. It was Slava with a girl, whom he introduced as Larisa. She was about twenty-one, pretty, with striking blue eyes set far apart in her oval face, well-shaped lips and long auburn hair hanging over her shoulders and down her back. She wore a dark green skirt, as short as was the rule in Moscow. She was clearly fashion conscious and extremely attractive.

'I have explained to Larisa, Robert, that you are a journalist from Britain who has come here to learn Russian.' After chatting for several minutes Slava said he had to go, and he went off leaving Larisa with Bourke.

'It is extremely kind of you to agree to help me,' Bourke began. 'Getting things like theatre tickets is difficult when you don't speak the language.'

'I imagine so,' she replied smiling. 'I shall certainly help you with things like that, and of course I am glad to have the opportunity to practise my English.' In fact her English was near perfect with only a trace of foreign accent. They talked for a couple of hours and she told Bourke that she was in the philological faculty of Moscow University, and besides English her languages were French, German and Norwegian. Her home was in the Urals where her mother was a doctor and divorced from her father who was a history lecturer. Later they had dinner together in the hotel and Bourke saw her back to the university hostel in a taxi.

Thereafter they met every day and developed an intimate personal

---

[1] Donald Maclean was the British diplomat who defected to the Soviet Union with Guy Burgess in 1951. The CIA particularly disliked him because they suspected him of giving atomic secrets to the Russians when he was working in the British Embassy in Washington during the war. His wife Melinda subsequently married Philby as his fourth wife. Maclean died in Moscow in 1983, aged sixty-nine.

relationship. Bourke felt he had to be honest with her. He told her about Blake, Stan and Slava, explaining that the latter did not belong to Intourist but like Stan was a KGB officer. In due course Stan and Slava found out, but they did not seem to mind particularly, merely asking Larisa not to discuss Bourke with her fellow students apart from the fact that he was a visiting British journalist.

On Christmas Eve Stan rang up Bourke to wish him a happy Christmas under the impression that it was Christmas Day. When Bourke told him it was next day, Stan invited him to lunch 'to celebrate'. Bourke was surprised at the disappearance of Christmas in the Soviet curriculum, Christmas trees being called New Year trees and Father Christmas 'Father 1968'. In the Soviet Union at that time Christmas Day was an ordinary working day and Stan had never known any otherwise, having been brought up on Marx's precept that religion was 'the opium of the people'.

During the meal Stan was so subdued that Bourke asked him whether there was anything on his mind. When Stan said there was not, Bourke remarked, 'I thought you might be worried that I might do something to detract from the glory of this Philby business.'

This period coincided with the fiftieth anniversary of the foundation of the Tcheka, predecessor of the KGB, by Felix Dzerzhinsky. The occasion was exploited by the Government organ *Izvestia* in the shape of a detailed account of the achievements of Kim Philby, who worked for the KGB and reputedly acted as political adviser to Andropov. Like Blake, Philby had been awarded the Order of Lenin and also the Order of the Red Banner, and he was enthusiastically lauded in *Izvestya* in what was a striking propaganda exercise by the KGB.

Stan's face lit up at Bourke's words. 'Well, now that you come to mention it, Seán,' he said, 'I would appreciate it if you would make a special effort to avoid causing us any embarrassment in the next few weeks. It would be a pity if the other side were given an opportunity to see you at the moment.'

'Don't worry, Stan,' Bourke assured the KGB officer. 'I shall be very careful. I don't begrudge you your little victory.' With that they shook hands, the relief plainly showing on Stan's features.

By the middle of January 1968, Bourke's new flat was still not ready, and Larisa suggested that as a change from the boredom of hotel life they should go off for a fortnight's skiing in the country putting up at a university guest house. Bourke thought this was an excellent idea, but he had first to clear it with Stan. Fortunately Stan was agreeable and so off they went by train to Mozhaisk, about fifty miles west of Moscow on the line to Smolensk. At Mozhaisk station a bus belonging to the university took them to the guest house a short distance away in a small village called Krasnovidova. Two adjacent rooms were reserved for Bourke and Larisa and they had a table to themselves in the dining room. The presence of a foreigner caused quite a stir and Larisa was constantly explaining that her companion was an English journalist studying Russian. There was no doubt, too, that Larisa was the best-looking girl in the place. As she came into the dining room in a tight-fitting red blouse and jeans, Bourke could hear others at neighbouring tables saying '*Krasivaya devushka!*' (What a pretty girl!)

Larisa was also a good pianist and could sing well. When she was at the piano in the recreation room, a crowd of envious males would gather round. But when the performance was over, Larisa would talk to them politely and then make her way to where Bourke was standing and put her arm through his thus making it clear that she belonged to him. It made him feel good.

Once when they were skiing together in the forest nearby, she paused to take off her fur hat to adjust her hair, when a group of other skiers passed by and the woman in the lead looked at Larisa. 'My goodness,' she said, 'that girl is beautiful. She looks like the Mona Lisa!'

'Did you hear what she said?' Bourke asked Larisa.

'Yes, but she doesn't know much about art, does she?'

'I think she knows a lot about art,' said Bourke as he glanced at his companion.

On another occasion they danced together in the snow. 'You know, Seán,' said Larisa, 'if anyone saw us now they would think we were mad.'

'And perhaps they wouldn't be far wrong,' said Bourke to the girl in his arms. 'But what a nice kind of madness!' As they danced he sang a song, 'Love me tenderly'. And that no doubt is what she did, since they were now sleeping together.

At the end of the fortnight they returned to Moscow. And while Larisa went off to the Urals to spend the remainder of the New Year vacation with her mother, Seán Bourke went back to the Warsaw Hotel. Drink was his solace for missing Larisa, and, four days after his return to the hotel, he had a long lunch in the hotel restaurant where he drank several bottles of wine and most of a bottle of brandy.

Fortified and emboldened by this liquor, he went back to his room, determined to try and get in touch with his brother Kevin in Scotland. He picked up the telephone.

'*Da?*' said the operator.

'*Ya. Angleesky.*'

'Oh, you are English?'

'Yes. I am. I would like to make a call to Britain, a town in Scotland called Ayr. The number is Ayr 65410.'

'It will take about an hour. Goodbye.'

Seán Bourke did not think he would get away with it and fully expected a knock on the door and someone from the KGB coming in to cancel the call. But no such thing happened. In just about an hour the phone rang. Bourke picked up the receiver, and heard an English operator's voice. 'You're through to Ayr. Go ahead.'

'Is that you, Kevin?'

'Yes. It is.'

'This is Seán here, calling from Moscow.'

'Listen, Seán. It's a great relief to hear your voice. We thought we'd never hear from you again. In fact, we thought you had been liquidated.'

'Why did you think that?'

'Well, those reports in the papers about your going to the British Embassy. The rumour here was that you had been definitely shot for doing that. I've had the Special Branch along to see me several times. An Inspector told me that they knew for sure that you had been locked up in the Lubyanka after your visit to the embassy.'

'None of that is true, Kevin. On the contrary, I was sent on a tour of the Soviet Union. Actually from the material point of view I am very well off here. I do no work and I get £30 a week.'

'And you still want to come back?'

'Yes, I do. I've made up my mind about that.'

'But listen, Seán. The Special Branch have told me you'll get at least fifteen years. The authorities here are very angry with you.'

'I shall return to Ireland and fight extradition on the grounds that Blake was a political prisoner.'

'You can forget about that. The Special Branch have told me that your extradition from Ireland is a foregone conclusion. They say it has already been tied up with the Irish authorities.'

'That's an insult to the Irish judiciary. Extradition is a matter for the judges, not policemen. Can you imagine an Irish judge being a tool of Scotland Yard?'

'But supposing you *are* extradited under Irish law?'

'That's a chance I am quite prepared to take.'

'OK, Seán, that's up to you. I just thought I should warn you, that's all.'

'Thanks. Listen, Kevin. There are a few things I should like to clear up *before* I return. I would like your help here. Do you think you could come and visit me here in Moscow this summer?'

'I'd like to. In fact, I was going to suggest it.'

'Good. We'll discuss the dates and routes by letter.'

They said goodbye after Seán had promised Kevin to write in a week and warned him that their telephone call was being tapped both in Moscow and London.

It was a Saturday and Seán thought he would hear something by Monday. But not a word. On Tuesday Slava came to lunch at the hotel but did not mention the telephone call. So to allay his anxiety, Seán decided to call Stan direct at his office in Dzerzhinsky Square. 'I have a bit of news for you,' he opened the conversation. 'Would you be surprised to hear that on Saturday night I spoke by telephone to my brother Kevin in Scotland?'

'Yes, Seán,' answered Stan after a brief silence. 'I *would* be surprised and disappointed.'

'Well, I have written a full transcript of our conversation for you.'

Stan was at the hotel in half-an-hour and lost no time in coming to the point. 'We have been trying for months to convince the British that you had left the Soviet Union,' he told Bourke frankly, though he sounded annoyed. 'Your letter from Vienna was part of the process. Now they know again you are here. They will probably apply for you to be handed over and this will embarrass our Foreign Minister.'

'I'm sorry about that, Stan,' Bourke replied apologetically. 'But I've got problems of my own. I have had no contact with my family for more than a year and they didn't know what had happened to me. I have a duty to them, too, you know.'

'Yes, I know that, Seán. But if you had discussed it with me I could have helped you. We could have made some arrangement. This way you are causing everyone a lot of embarrassment – including me.'

'There really isn't much to worry about,' said Bourke, handing Stan the transcript. 'What transpired between Kevin and myself can't embarrass anyone except the British. As you will see, I reassured him that I was being treated with great courtesy and consideration in this country.'

'Seán, I wish, when you have a problem like this, you would discuss it with your friends – with Slava or me or George.'

'Blake!' Bourke exclaimed. 'George Blake is no friend of mine, Stan. I respect you and I respect Slava, but I have no respect at all for George Blake – so let us not talk about him.'

'Yes, I had heard that relations between you were unsatisfactory,' said Stan. 'That's a pity.' As he got up to leave, he added: 'Well, I sincerely hope, Seán, that you regard *me* as a friend.'

'I certainly do, Stan', Bourke replied, holding out his hand which Stan shook warmly.

Before he left, Stan told Bourke that now it was known where he was, since he had given his brother the name of the hotel, foreign newspaper correspondents would undoubtedly try to contact him. Hence a KGB guard would be posted in the lobby to see that he was not disturbed until he was moved into his new flat.

A few days later Slava arrived in a car and took Bourke and his luggage to the flat, a spacious and comfortable one. It had three rooms besides a kitchen and bathroom. This was indeed a great privilege, since a flat of this kind would normally be occupied by a family of six. Even Stan, a KGB colonel, regarded as single, was restricted to one room in a flat which he shared.

8

Seán Bourke spent his days in the flat engaged in writing his account of the escape from Wormwood Scrubs and his experiences in the Soviet Union, a work which was to develop into a book which he called *The Springing of George Blake*. He wrote in exercise books and when he was expecting a visit from Stan or Slava he would hide them in a suitcase under his bed. He did not tell the KGB what he was doing since his writing contained pertinent criticisms of Blake and his behaviour, and he hoped to smuggle the manuscript out of the country when it was finished. The evenings he spent mostly with Larisa. He also wrote regularly to his brother Kevin, leaving the envelopes unsealed to save the KGB the trouble of steaming them open in Dzerzhinsky Square. It was arranged that Kevin should come to Moscow and stay with Seán in August, and the KGB undertook to see that he was given a visa in London without any awkward questions.

Larisa did not like going out to restaurants, but was pleased to go to the cinema or theatre with Seán or for a walk in a nearby park. Most of the time, however, she spent in the flat talking or making love. She was as ardent a Communist as her lover was a capitalist. 'Heavens, Seán,' she said on one occasion when Seán's arguments had brought her near to tears, 'if you knew anything at all about our history you wouldn't say terrible things like that. If you had any idea of the suffering and misery and degradation that our people had to endure before the Revolution, you wouldn't be so ready to condemn us now. Today in this country we enjoy a freedom and dignity that our parents and grandparents never dreamed of. I am proud of my country and am prepared to die for it if necessary.'

The university summer vacation lasted for two months and they decided to spend half or more of it together, Larisa going to her mother's in the Urals for the remainder. Seán told her that he preferred not to stay in a hotel or a sanatorium. This decision suited Larisa. 'Personally,' she said, 'I would love to stay in a tiny cottage somewhere remote where we can go swimming and walking and fishing and I can do the cooking.'

Bourke put the idea to the KGB and it was approved since Mrs Blake was paying another visit to her son in July, and it would be desirable if there was no chance of her seeing Bourke. Slava undertook to make the necessary arrangements. As a result they flew from Moscow by Ilyushin jet to Minsk, the capital of Byelorussia, where they were met by a local KGB officer called Alexander. He took them to a biplane which flew them on to a small town called Braslav, some two hundred miles north of Minsk near the border with Lithuania. 'Our roads in Byelorussia are not too good,' Alexander explained. 'All our towns, large and small, are connected by these biplanes. They are our buses.' The airstrip was about a couple of miles from Braslav and here they were met by Valentin, a young KGB officer, who drove them in a jeep along a mud track to a secluded log cabin beside a lake, while Alexander, after seeing them settled in, caught the next plane back to Minsk and Valentin arranged with the nearby collective farm to supply the couple with fresh food and milk daily. Thereafter Valentin would call once a week to see that they had everything they needed. What struck Bourke particularly was that in a relatively small district like Braslav there should be two KGB officers. As he noted, the tentacles of Dzerzhinsky Square spread far.

It was a delightful situation by the lake where Seán and Larisa spent five blissful weeks. The scenery was superb, and in the evenings they would sit on the veranda sipping champagne and watch the sunset while Larisa sang Russian songs. Once when Seán had a cold Larisa went to the farm and brought back a jar of fresh honey and milk, stirring them together and spoon-feeding Seán with this delicious mixture to which from time to time she added more honey.

Towards the end of their stay the question of Seán's return to Ireland came up. They had often discussed this in the past. Larisa knew how he felt but still hoped to dissuade him. They were lying side by side at the edge of the lake sunbathing, Larisa's beautiful long hair spread out on the grass round her shoulders.

'Seán,' she said anxiously, 'they'll put you in prison and they might even beat you. I can't bear to think of that.'

'I've told you before, Larisa, I think I've a good chance of getting away with it in Ireland. As for being beaten, even if I get sent back to Britain I don't think that will happen. Britain's not a police state.'

'Why can't you stay, Seán, why? We could be so happy together. This is a big country, a beautiful country. We could go anywhere, live anywhere, do anything. Why do you have to leave?'

'Because, Larisa, I have to be sure I am free.'

'But you *are* free, Seán, you *are*. You are not being kept here against your will.'

'I must be sure of that, Larisa, for my own peace of mind. And the only way I can be sure is by putting it to the test. I will never know whether I am free to leave this country unless I actually leave. That is the *only* way I will know.'

'But you've got everything here.'

'I know that, but no matter how well off I might be here, no matter what comforts are lavished on me, there would always be that doubt, that uncertainty. Can't you see that? I would be in a limbo, like Blake and Philby and Maclean. They are not happy in their enforced exile, and they actually *fought* for the Soviet Communist cause. I have to return to normality, even at the cost of going to prison.'

Larisa looked at her lover through tearful eyes. 'Perhaps we'll meet again when all this is over,' Seán said, taking her head in his hands, stroking her hair and trying to comfort her. But it was no good. He felt her tears on his chest. She was inconsolable.

The holiday ended on the last day of July when Valentin called for them in his jeep and drove them along the mud track to the Braslav airstrip where the biplane was waiting to take them to Minsk. Alexander met them when the biplane touched down there and they shared a bottle of champagne with him as they waited for the jet to Moscow. Stan was at Domodedova airport and drove them the thirty miles along the Kashira Highway to Seán's flat in the city.

The following evening Seán took Larisa to Kazan railway station and after a last fond farewell saw her on the train for the forty-eight hour journey to her mother's house in the Urals.

On 9 August, Blake telephoned Bourke and asked him to join him for a drink at the Moskva Hotel. There they spent a couple of hours drinking champagne cocktails. Blake, who was most friendly, explained that his mother had gone back to Holland, and he invited Bourke to his flat for supper. He was extremely attentive to Bourke throughout, since he realized that once Kevin had arrived there was nothing to prevent the details of his treatment of Seán reaching the West.

'Well, I hope that you and your brother have a very nice time,' said Blake as he showed him out of the flat. 'I'm sure we will,' said Seán who sensed from the look on Blake's face that in spite of his outward show of friendliness he bitterly resented the KGB's actions. In the event it was to be the last time that the two men met.

The Aftermath

I

KEVIN BOURKE'S visit to his brother was financed by the Sunday paper, the *News of the World*, in return for two articles describing Blake's escape from prison and his subsequent activities in hiding in England and later in the Soviet Union. Kevin arrived at Sheremetyevo International Airport at 5.30 pm on 12 August 1968. As soon as he had disembarked and entered the airport arrival lounge, he was approached by a man in a long blue raincoat who asked if he was Mr Bourke – it was probably Victor of the KGB. On replying that he was, the man said: 'I have been instructed to tell you that your brother will be here in about an hour.' Within the hour another man arrived. He turned out to be Stan, who introduced himself as a KGB colonel and explained to Kevin that Seán was waiting outside in case there were any foreign newspaper correspondents in the airport who might recognize him. Fortunately there were none.

Stan chatted with Kevin for a few minutes, making it clear that it was not until after Blake's escape that he (Blake) had any contact with the Russians. Afterwards Kevin admitted to the *News of the World*: 'The KGB colonel told me they were very surprised when Blake escaped from prison. They thought that the Czechs were behind it! They were in fact as worried as the British Special Branch, wondering who had Blake in the two months after the escape.'

As he left the airport lounge with Stan, Kevin saw a man wearing dark glasses. It was his brother. 'Sorry about these,' said Seán indicating the glasses. 'They are just a precaution. I did not know who might be about when you arrived.'

Stan took them in a chauffeur-driven car to Seán's flat where he stayed for one drink, promising to take them out to lunch next day. 'I hope you enjoy your stay in Moscow,' he told Kevin, adding that he would put a car at the brothers' disposal during the week that Kevin planned to be there.

Although the flat was on the eighth floor of a seemingly endless block of flats, Kevin was most impressed by the interior. There were paintings on the walls, and a rich red carpet on the living-room floor. The furniture was modern and of good quality. While they were talking about the events of the escape and filling in the gaps in each other's knowledge since they had last met, there was a ring at the front door bell. Seán made no move to answer it. There was another ring and still Seán did not move. 'I only answer when there are three short rings together,' he explained. 'That way I know it is a friend. Only the KGB, Blake and my housekeeper know the procedure. It's a precaution I have to take. I have heard that the American CIA are very eager to get hold of me.'

When they met, Kevin did not know that his brother had sprung Blake from Wormwood Scrubs until Seán enlightened him. 'Why do you think I have got all this?' he asked looking round the room. 'Because the Russians like the colour of my eyes? I do no work, although I could have a job if I wanted it. I could be an editor in a publishing house, but at the moment I prefer to relax. I have this flat rent free, and my gas, electricity, heating and telephone are also free. I even have a housekeeper. On top of all this I am given £30 a week pocket money. When you consider that a doctor or an engineer only gets about £15 I am very well off. In fact I live here as a highly privileged citizen.'

Kevin also noted traces of Larisa in the flat, her favourite teddy bear in the bedroom and her skiing equipment neatly stacked in the bathroom.

In due course Seán produced the nine exercise books in which he had written what was the manuscript of his book. 'Kevin,' he began, 'the main purpose of your visit, as I see it, is to take this story back to Britain with you. Although your presence here in Moscow will also increase my chances of getting out of here, I at least want to have the consolation of knowing that the truth has reached the outside world.'

'Oh, the truth about what?'

'The truth about George Blake.' Seán then proceeded to give his brother a detailed account of Blake's treachery. 'So you see,' he concluded, 'Blake repaid me for rescuing him from Wormwood Scrubs by trying to have me murdered!'

'Why, for God's sake, should he want to do that?'

'Because, Kevin, he is a born traitor. Blake does not betray for ideals. He betrays because he *needs* to betray. If Blake had been born a Russian, he would have betrayed the KGB to the British. That's how he's made.'

Kevin picked up the first exercise book and flicked through the pages. 'How will I get these out of the Soviet Union?' he asked.

'With the help of the KGB,' Seán told him. 'You are not an ordinary tourist. You are a privileged visitor. Stan will make arrangements for the formalities at the airport to be waived. Just put the exercise books at the bottom of your suitcase and there will be no trouble.'

'Right, I'll do that. By the way, where is Blake now?'

'Up to three days ago he was in the flat I shared with him when I first came to Moscow, but by now he will have been moved.'

'Why is that.'

'Secret service policy – in *every* country. It is assumed that when once an individual comes under the control of the other side, every secret he possesses will be divulged. I have contacted you and you are going back to Britain, and therefore it is assumed that Blake's address will be known to the British. So Blake has to move. It is automatic.'

Next day Stan took the two brothers to lunch at the fashionable and expensive Khimki Riverport restaurant. It was a lavish meal with caviare, smoked salmon, chicken, vodka, champagne and brandy. 'You must remember that Seán has rendered us a great service,' said Stan to Kevin, 'and we are extremely grateful to him. We feel it our duty to do everything we can to help him. But if he wants to go we'll guarantee to get him back to Ireland without touching England en route.' They went on to discuss various routes for reaching Ireland and how Kevin could help.

'All you have to do, Kevin,' said Seán, 'is to apply to the Irish Embassy in London for an Irish passport or other travel document on my behalf and then send it on to me. They can't refuse because I'm an Irish citizen.'

'With food and drink like this,' said Kevin, 'I'm surprised you want to leave at all.'

'I'm surprised too,' Stan said, 'but not because of the food and drink. I'm surprised that Seán wants to take the terrible risk. I honestly believe there is a good chance he will be handed over to the British and they will charge him under the Official Secrets Act and give him fifteen or twenty years. Believe me, Kevin, I am only concerned with Seán's welfare. We have nothing to lose by all this but he has.'

'And would he still be welcome to stay here now?' asked Kevin.

'More than welcome,' Stan assured him. 'I know that Seán is not a Communist, I know that he even dislikes our system, but nobody here minds about that. We've never made any attempt to convert him and we never will. He is welcome to stay here and he can have his free flat and £30 a week for the rest of his life. And he doesn't even have to work. He is better off than I am. I can assure you that if I stopped working nobody would pay me a penny. But anyway, the decision is entirely Seán's. If he wants to return to Ireland, we will give him every assistance.'

Kevin Bourke spent the remainder of his stay sightseeing and reading the manuscript of his brother's story. Seán had agreed with Stan that they should both see him off at Sheremetyevo Airport, and Stan arrived with a car and driver in the early afternoon which Stan reckoned should give Kevin plenty of time to catch the plane, check-in time being five o'clock. Seán carried Kevin's suitcase down in the lift to find the car outside with the driver, who had raised the bonnet, peering at the engine as if something was wrong. However, he greeted the three passengers as Seán put the suitcases in the boot and having wiped his hands on a cloth got into the driver's seat with Stan beside him and Kevin sat in the back.

They soon crossed the Ring Road and headed towards Shere-metyevo airport, a trip which normally takes about three-quarters of an hour. Several minor roads had to be negotiated before reaching the main highway and a delay of half an hour occurred on one of these when a level-crossing gate was down while a queue of traffic built up on either side. The cause of the delay turned out to be a single engine which took only a minute or two to cross the road. 'A little matter of mixed priorities here,' said Seán to Stan who smiled and shrugged his shoulders. Such delays were, and still are, not uncommon in the Soviet Union. Meanwhile Kevin looked anxiously at his watch. 'I've got to check in by five,' he said. 'It's now half past four.'

'Don't worry, Kevin,' said Stan. 'You'll make it. We'll take a short cut.' He said a few words in Russian to the driver and they turned off on to a dual carriageway, where there was not much traffic. They made good going for the next twenty minutes when the engine began to splutter and the driver pulled into the side of the road. The driver pressed the accelerator but the vehicle refused to move. They all got out, the driver lifted the bonnet and poked around inside. He then spoke to Stan who said to the other two: 'I'm afraid, boys, there is some trouble with the distributor, but it shouldn't take too long to fix.'

Kevin looked at his watch. It was five o'clock, the time he was supposed to check in. 'Don't worry, Kevin,' Seán reassured him. 'Five o'clock is the *earliest* time you have to check in, but I'm sure they'll let you check in by half-past five at least.' Stan confirmed this, and Kevin remarked that he hoped they were right as his wife was expecting him in London that night and would be very upset if he failed to appear.

By ten past five the driver had not succeeded in repairing the distributor and Kevin was becoming agitated. 'How far are we from the airport?' asked Seán. 'About twenty minutes' drive' was the reply. 'Can't you use your car radio to call up the airport and ask for help?' Unfortunately this was not possible, since the car did not have a radio.

'In that case we had better stop a taxi,' said Kevin. But Stan explained that they had taken a short cut and, the carriageway not being the direct route to the airport, there were unlikely to be any taxis. However, at 5.25 a taxi did appear and Stan stopped it, at the same time beckoning Kevin and Seán to come over to it which they did. 'I'm afraid, boys' said Stan, 'there is only room for one, so it looks as if Kevin will have to go to the airport alone.' Seán looked inside the taxi, and sure enough there were three other passengers and there was only room for one more.

Accordingly Kevin's case was transferred to the taxi's boot. Kevin said his good-byes and then clambered into the taxi. 'All the best, Kevin,' said his brother. 'See you in Ireland one of these days!' After he had gone Stan said he thought Kevin should make it all right. 'What a pity!' he went on. 'I would have liked to have been at the airport to usher Kevin through without the usual formalities.'

Meanwhile the driver worked on at the distributor and eventually it functioned again and the engine started up. By this time it was six o'clock. 'No point in going to the airport now,' said Stan. 'I think we should go back to town and I'll go to the office and telephone the airport from there. I'll drop you off at your flat first and give you a ring later when I've found out what has happened.' At the same time he berated the driver. 'As you know,' he said to Seán, 'drivers in this country are also mechanics and are responsible for the maintenance of their vehicles. He should have checked the engine thoroughly before we left Moscow.' As we have seen, he did so and apparently was not satisfied with it, but decided to take a chance.

They returned to the city and Seán was dropped at his flat. The phone there rang at 7.30. It was Stan. 'Well, Seán,' he said. 'I phoned the airport and Kevin caught his flight all right.'

'That's a relief,' observed Seán. 'No snags?'

'No, everything is all right. He's on his way to London.' Seán put the receiver down and heaved a sigh of relief. From what Stan had said, it looked as if the manuscript was also on its way to London.

2

A week later Larisa returned to Moscow from seeing her mother and brought several jars of honey and mushrooms from the Urals. She and Seán had a quiet reunion celebration in his flat with champagne and caviare and she cooked a Urals speciality called *pelmeni*, a kind of ravioli which they both enjoyed. As usual they slept together for she was still very much in love with her Irish boyfriend and dreaded his leaving the Soviet Union.

Stan phoned several times during the week and Slava called at the flat to give Seán copies of *The Times* and to talk about his return to Ireland. Seán rang Blake several times but never got any reply so that it was clear he had been moved. In fact he was on holiday on the Black Sea.

On 3 September, fifteen days after Kevin's departure, the phone rang at the flat. It was Stan. 'Hello, Seán,' he said. Then, after a pause he went on: 'It appears that your manuscript was taken from Kevin at the airport. It is a great pity that you did not ask *us* to arrange for it to be sent to Britain. We could have helped you in this matter.' He spoke quietly and without a trace of resentment, although he made it clear that he disagreed with much of what Seán had written. 'It is a pity you hold these views, but as I told my colleagues there is no point in trying to deprive you of the manuscript because you can simply rewrite the whole thing when you get back to Ireland.' Also Stan felt that he was 'completely wrong' about George Blake. 'Still, if that's your view you are, of course, entitled to your opinion.' He added that Slava would be coming along to see him at the flat that evening and would talk about it.

How did the KGB know that Kevin had the manuscript? So Seán asked himself, and he concluded that there was only one answer – the flat was bugged and Seán's conversation with his brother had been recorded. This was the third time that Seán Bourke had annoyed the KGB – first, by going to the British Embassy in Moscow, secondly by telephoning Kevin in Scotland, and thirdly by trying to use Kevin to smuggle the manuscript out of the country.

He wondered if his luck would hold out and if he would be allowed to leave the Soviet Union.

Slava called at the flat as Stan said he would. He brought with him a letter from Kevin which he handed to Seán. It had been posted the day after Kevin's return to London and normally it should have taken ten days to reach Seán. But in this case it took fourteen which implied that the KGB wished to finish reading the controversial manuscript before handing over the letter, which must inevitably refer to what had happened at the airport. It was brief and in it Kevin expressed concern for his brother's safety. It also contained a passage which was obviously meant for the eyes of the KGB.

I have, of course, read the manuscript word for word and know all the things you said about Blake. My advice to you is to come back to Ireland and not bother to write anything. Forget all about Blake and I will do the same.

'He is obviously worried about me,' Seán told Slava. 'Perhaps I should get in touch with him straight away and reassure him.'

'Why not telephone him?' Slava responded. 'Tomorrow I shall find out the code number that you have to dial from a flat to get through to the foreign exchange and you can phone him tomorrow night.'

Slava was obviously upset about the manuscript, but like Stan he showed neither anger nor resentment. 'It is a pity you have this opinion of our country,' he said, 'and it is a pity you write these terrible things about Blake.' So he had read it too. When Seán asked him where the manuscript was and when he was likely to get it back, Slava told him that the Customs had passed it on to the Press Committee to consider. 'That is the law,' he explained. 'The Press Committee have to examine all written material leaving the Soviet Union. It has nothing to do with the KGB. When the Press Committee have finished with your manuscript you'll get it back.' This was a face-saving exercise since Seán knew that the manuscript was in Dzerzhinsky Square. Otherwise how could Slava and Stan have read it?

Slava duly gave Seán the foreign exchange code number and with this Seán was duly able to phone Kevin who was greatly relieved to hear his voice since he thought his brother was in serious trouble with the KGB. 'We were all very worried about you here. That business on the way to the airport was all fixed. The breakdown was phoney and the taxi was phoney. And what's more your flat is bugged. It was all a fix!'

'But Kevin, the Customs *have* to take manuscripts and pass them on to the Press Committee. That's the law of the land.'

'Customs? What do you mean, Customs? The KGB were waiting for me at the airport. The moment I put my case on the Customs counter a young man in civilian clothes who was standing behind the Customs officer said, "Oh, we have a special room for you. Follow me." He took me to a room at the back of the Customs and tore my luggage apart. And then he *searched me* – every pocket and even my wallet. He took your manuscript and my own notebook and went into another room. Five minutes later he returned and gave me back my notebook. "This is yours," he said, "you can have this. The exercise books we must keep." My opinion is that when he went into the second room he showed all the stuff to someone who was able to tell him exactly what to give back to me and what to keep. The man in the other room must have been someone who is known to you, someone who even knows your handwriting. Perhaps it was Slava or Victor, or even Blake himself.'

'Well,' said Seán, 'I shall pass your remarks on to Stan and see what he says.'

'Yes, do that,' replied Kevin. 'And are they still going to send you back to Ireland?'

'Of course. Why shouldn't they?'

'I hope you're right. If their intentions towards you are so honourable, why do they play tricks like this?'

'You still can't be sure it *was* a trick' was Seán's comment on his brother's account. 'I consider Stan and Slava to be my friends and there is no doubt in my mind that they will arrange my return to Ireland.'

'I just hope you're right,' said Kevin, 'I've been in touch with the Irish Embassy in London and you will have a travel document in a couple of weeks. And don't forget to tell Stan what I've said.'

'I'll do that.'

So he did. He also wrote a transcript of his telephone conversation and passed it to Slava. Both Slava and Stan rejected the suggestion that there was anything phoney about the journey to the airport, and on balance they may well have been right, particularly in the light of Stan's reprimanding the driver for his negligence in not satisfying himself before they started that the car was completely roadworthy.

A month passed and there was no sign of the manuscript which Seán Bourke had been expecting to be returned to him. However, he was not unduly concerned, since, as Stan had surmised, he could always rewrite it at home. Meanwhile Stan and Slava were being very attentive to him and constantly invited him for meals at expensive restaurants and would sometimes reserve a private room at the Metropole. On these occasions they would talk about the manuscript, suggesting that perhaps Bourke had misunderstood Blake's words and intentions. What concerned the KGB officers was Bourke's attitude to Blake. Bourke's adverse criticisms of the Soviet Union and Soviet life did not worry them, or if it did they did not show it. Thus Seán Bourke found himself admiring these two men for their 'unswerving loyalty to Blake and for their tenacious efforts to defend him'. He also found himself 'contrasting them as individuals with the traitor whom they were compelled by duty to support'.

3

Seán Bourke's travel document arrived on 10 October 1968. It was issued by the Irish Republic's Embassy in London and was valid for one month and for one journey from Moscow to Ireland 'by the most direct route'. It was agreed with the KGB that he should leave Moscow eleven days later, on 21 October and travel to Dublin via Amsterdam. On 17 October Stan took him out to lunch at the Arbat restaurant, beginning eating and drinking at two o'clock and not finishing until ten. Bourke had got used to the KGB habit of not raising any possibly unpleasant question on such occasions without leading up to it slowly and gradually. Bourke wondered what it would be this time.

'I think, Seán,' said Stan at 9.00 pm, 'it would be a good idea if you left your manuscript behind and when you have arrived safely in Ireland we can send it on to you. If you take it yourself you might be arrested when you arrive in Dublin and the manuscript confiscated.' Seán agreed that this made sense, adding that he was content to leave the matter in Stan's hands.

On the evening before his departure they had a farewell dinner in the flat. Seán and Larisa acted as hosts to Stan and Slava. Slava produced Seán's air ticket together with exit visa and 40 American dollars. 'You have a two-hour wait at Schipol airport at Amsterdam and you then catch your connecting flight to Dublin,' Slava told him. 'You don't have to go through immigration at Amsterdam so there should be no difficulty in changing planes. I think 40 dollars should be enough for the journey, don't you?'

'More than enough, Slava,' Bourke replied. 'Many thanks.'

Shortly afterwards the phone rang in the hall and Seán excused himself to answer it. It was Kevin asking for confirmation of next day's flight. 'Yes,' he told his brother. 'Everything has been arranged. I'll be in Amsterdam about midday, as I've told you.'

'Good,' Kevin answered. 'I'll be waiting for you in Dublin. I've taken the precaution of telling the press that you are coming. I think the more people who know about it the more likely you are to arrive.'

'A very wise move. Thank you.'

'I've also arranged with Granada to meet you in Amsterdam. The man who will approach you is a reporter with a programme called "World in Action". I've told him that you will be carrying a copy of *Pravda*.'

'OK. I'll remember that.'

'See you in Dublin.'

'Yes indeed.'

After Seán had come back to the table, Stan said he would call in the morning to collect him and Larisa and drive them to the Sheremetyevo airport, since Larisa also naturally wanted to see him off. Since Seán would not be seeing Slava again, they said good-bye in the flat, Slava shaking his hand warmly. 'I wish you every success, Seán, and I hope we meet again.' Slava and Stan then left the flat.

Seán and Larisa went to bed together – for the last time. Next morning after breakfast and while waiting for Stan, Larisa opened her handbag and took out a plain gold ring. 'Until we meet again, Seán,' she said as she slipped the ring on the third finger of his right hand. Her lover was dumbfounded with gratitude, since he knew that she must have queued for hours to get it.

Stan arrived, this time with a car in perfect mechanical order. Seán's luggage consisted only of a briefcase containing a clean shirt and underwear, a pair of socks and a little green toy dog Larisa had given him when he was staying at the Warsaw Hotel and which squeaked as it was pressed. All Seán's other belongings he left behind in the flat.

As the airport came into sight, Stan said something to the driver who then slowed down. 'I think you should say good-bye some little distance from the terminal entrance,' he said, turning to the others. 'There might be news correspondents there, and Larisa and I should not be photographed. Oh, and by the way, Seán, if you see me in the departure lounge after you have checked in, pretend you don't know me.'

The car stopped about a hundred yards from the terminal building, and the three got out. Seán shook hands with Stan, who said goodbye, adding, 'And remember you are free to turn back right up to the moment the plane takes off.' Seán then embraced Larisa, and after a long, last kiss she said, 'I'll be up on the balcony to watch you go.'

Seán thereupon passed through the departures entrance. He checked in, filling up the Customs form he was given and stating that he had nothing to declare. He handed the form to the woman Customs officer together with his travel document and exit visa. 'Have you any foreign currency?' the Customs woman asked.

'Yes. Forty dollars.'

'Then why didn't you declare it?' she asked aggressively.

'Well . . .' Bourke began but was interrupted by a man standing next to her who glanced at his exit visa and whispered something in her ear. She immediately handed him back his papers without another word.

Bourke climbed the stairs to the departure lounge and as he had to wait for half an hour before the flight departure was called he went along to the bar for a drink, which he bought and carried to a table where he sat down. Five minutes later Stan appeared and also bought a drink, sitting at a nearby table. Seán pretended to ignore him as he had been instructed, but he could see that Stan was carefully scrutinizing the other passengers. Seán got up when the rest of the flight was called and walked towards the departure gate. Stan appeared nearby and as they passed each other, without turning his head Stan muttered in a barely audible whisper, 'Goodbye, Seán. Good luck!' To which Seán replied, repeating his thanks.

At passport control a young frontier guard was openly photographing the passengers on the flight as they passed. Bourke knew that this was not normal routine and he could not but help admire the KGB for their thoroughness. The guard in the control box looked carefully at Bourke's papers and handed back the travel document but kept the exit visa which was on a separate sheet of paper. He then pulled back the metal barrier to let Seán pass, and he had to wait on the other side until all the passengers had been correctly processed. Another guard then escorted the passengers in a group across the thirty yards of tarmac to the Aeroflot plane, which was waiting. Seán looked back at the terminal building and saw Larisa on the balcony, her auburn hair blowing in the breeze. She waved and he waved back. He then waited to be the last passenger to board the aircraft and at the top of the steps he turned round and gave one last wave before going inside.

Most of the other passengers were American tourists, loudly talking about their experiences in the Soviet Union. Traffic control gave the signal, the Ilyushin jet taxied down the runway and took off for the west. The flight was uneventful and arrived on time at Amsterdam where Seán Bourke was due to change planes.

4

As he entered the arrival lounge at Schipol airport in Amsterdam, a young man came up to him and inquired: 'Excuse me, are you Mr Bourke?'

'I am.'

'Oh, good. I'm from Granada Television. Your brother told me that you were expecting to meet me.'

'That's right.'

'Well, we'd like to do an interview. Would you care to come along to our hotel?'

'I'd love to.'

At passport control the Dutch immigration officer briefly glanced at Bourke's travel document and waved him through the barrier. Bourke as an Irish national did not require a visa to enter the Netherlands.

The television team had their cameras ready at the hotel and the interview duly took place. Presently the telephone rang. It was Kevin who asked to speak to his brother. 'Listen, Seán,' he said. 'There's a fog here in Dublin and planes are being diverted to London or Belfast.' Seán got the message all right and immediately cancelled his flight to Dublin.

He spent the night in Amsterdam and telephoned Kevin to let him know that he would fly Pan-American to Shannon airport in County Clare, about fifteen miles from Limerick on the other side of the river. Since there were then no direct flights from Amsterdam to Shannon, Seán Bourke flew with the Granada television team by British United Airways to Düsseldorf where he spent a couple of hours before transferring with the television crew to the Pan-American airliner bound for New York but stopping first at Shannon.

Four hours later, as the aircraft came down to land at Shannon, Seán Bourke could see the Clare Hills where he used to hide as a boy in the hay barns when he played truant from school and later when the police were looking for him for thieving. On landing the television camera men disembarked first so as to record Bourke's arrival, which they did against the background of quite a crowd since the arrival had been extensively publicized in advance. As he stepped on Irish soil, Seán Bourke recalled that the date was 22 October 1968, two years to the day since he engineered Blake's escape from Wormwood Scrubs.

From Shannon Bourke flew to Dublin where he put up at the Gresham Hotel pending his finding suitable permanent accommodation. Meanwhile, since his arrival had been widely noticed in the English as well as the Irish press, the British Foreign Office applied to the Attorney-General for Ireland and Commissioner of the Garda (Irish police) for an extradition order requiring the delivery of Seán Alphonsus Bourke to the authorities in London on the grounds that he had contrived to effect the escape of George Blake, a convicted criminal serving a sentence, from an English prison, in accordance with the terms of the existing Anglo-Irish treaty.

Seán Bourke was accordingly arrested at 6.00 am on 31 October at the Gresham Hotel. Later the same morning he appeared before the Dublin District Court where an order was made under the Irish Extradition Act of 1965 for his delivery to the British Special Branch. Bail was refused and he was taken to Mountjoy Prison there to await the arrival of the Special Branch officers. However, on the same day Bourke's solicitor issued High Court writs against the Attorney-General and the Garda Commission appealing against the extradition order, and Bourke was accordingly released pending the determination of the case in the Dublin High Court.

The case in which Bourke challenged the extradition order opened before Mr Justice O'Keefe, President of the Republic High Court, on 20 January 1969. It was preceded a week before by an order requiring the tapes of a television interview with Bourke by Radio Telefís Éirenn to be handed over to the court which was duly done. Mr Declan Costello, Senior Counsel, appeared at the hearing for Bourke, who began by stating that three friends had raised £800, of which £200 was used to 'spring' Blake from Wormwood Scrubs Prison, his counsel having argued that Blake must be regarded as a political prisoner, otherwise a prisoner of conscience. Asked by his counsel about his motives for his action, Bourke replied: 'I agreed to help George Blake to escape from prison because, first, I looked upon him as a political prisoner, who had sacrificed a great deal for what he believed in; secondly, because of his savage sentence which was the result of a trick by a very angry British Establishment; and thirdly, I felt great compassion for this man in his awful plight. There was one other consideration in my view, and it influenced my decision – as a result of many lengthy conversations with him I had come to the conclusion that his ideas of a just society coincided with my own.'

'Did Blake ask you to help him to escape? How did it come about?' Costello asked the plaintiff.

'Because he asked me,' Bourke replied.

'Were you aware that he had been convicted of spying for the Russian Government.'

'Yes.'

'Did you consider whether helping him to escape would help the Russians?'

'I appreciated that his escape would cause a great deal of embarrassment to the British Government,' Bourke replied to this question. 'I realized that as soon as Blake arrived as we planned, he would pass on . . .'

At this point Mr Niall McCarthy, SC, who appeared for the State, objected, and the judge ruled that he would not accept any further evidence of Blake's activities in the Soviet Union. The President said he would reserve judgement and the hearing was accordingly adjourned for a fortnight.

On 3 February, President O'Keefe refused to grant an extradition order and directed that the plaintiff should be released. 'I think that the offence of helping Blake can be called a political offence,' the President held. 'The evidence satisfies me that such assistance as the plaintiff gave towards the escape of George Blake was not given with a view to furthering the political aims of the Soviet Union.' The judge added that he regarded Bourke's reasons for helping Blake as being sufficient to make what would otherwise not be a political offence an offence of a political character. 'Blake's offences were clearly political offences. He was a political prisoner in the sense that he was in prison convicted of having committed a political offence.' Nor was there any evidence that Bourke was in favour of the Soviet or any Soviet bloc countries. It may be noted that the Irish Extradition Act had recently been amended to cover not merely a political offence but 'an offence connected with a political offence' and that was held by the President as the ground for refusing the extradition order.

The Irish Attorney-General gave notice of appeal against President O'Keefe's refusal to grant the extradition order. A warrant was accordingly issued for Bourke's arrest on 2 July and the hearing began before the Supreme Court on the following day, but was postponed since Bourke was suffering from a throat infection. In the event the Supreme Court upheld the High Court order and on 31 July extradition was refused.

Meanwhile, Bourke had further trouble with the law. On 3 July he was charged in the District Court with being drunk in charge of a firearm at Groome's Hotel in Dublin on 20 June, carrying a firearm (for his own protection, so he said) without a certificate and possessing an automatic pistol with six pounds of ammunition. Although this had been a capital offence in earlier days, Bourke seems to have got off lightly on this occasion, being discharged on probation.

At this period Bourke rented a flat in Leahy House, a block at Sandymount, a fashionable suburb a few miles south of the city centre overlooking Dublin Bay on the way to Blackrock and Dunleary. Here he rewrote that part of his book which covered his time in the Soviet Union and had not been returned to him by the KGB. *The Springing of George Blake* (incidentally dedicated to Larisa) was published in 1970 and not only did he sell the book rights but also the film and ancillary rights, from which he was said to have made something in the region of £40,000. One of his proudest possessions was a certificate from the Inland Revenue Commissioners exempting him from paying income tax on his literary earnings on the grounds that legally speaking he was an 'artist'. However, he spent most of his money on drink and extravagant living. During this period he met a Dutch nurse in Dublin with whom he had an affair, resulting in the birth of a daughter. His mistress later left him and went to France, taking their daughter with her.

After this Bourke returned to his native Limerick where he lived for a time in a converted grain store. About 1980, when he was already quite penurious, he considered surrendering himself to the British authorities in the hope that he would get off with a relatively short sentence. However, he changed his mind a little later and went to live at Kilkee, a pleasant seaside resort in County Clare, renowned for its bathing, reputedly the best in Ireland, which he had known as a boy. Here he began to write a book on the psychological approach of prisoners to long-term sentences. Unfortunately he did not live to finish it.

In the afternoon of 26 January 1982 he collapsed in the street and was helped into a near-by house by some kindly passers-by; but in spite of the efforts of two doctors to revive him he died two hours later. A post-mortem took place at the County Hospital on the following day when the cause of death was certified as 'acute pulmonary oedema, left ventricle failure, and coronary thrombosis'. He was aged forty-nine at the time of his death, which was not directly due to alcoholic poisoning, as has been incorrectly stated, although his drinking no doubt contributed to his disease.

5

On 17 February 1970 a leading article appeared in the London *Times* charging the Russians with being particularly rude to Britain when it suited them. An extract follows:

It is hard to think of anything ruder between two nations than for one of them to parade and honour the other's traitors. The Russians put Philby on show some time ago. Now they have let George Blake, the double spy, give his account of how he betrayed Britain time and again. His story has appeared in successive days in the Soviet Government's own official newspaper *Izvestia*. To cap it all came the news that Blake – who caused the death of many of his colleagues in the intelligence services – has been

awarded the Order of Lenin and the military Order of the Red
Banner. No clearer recognition could be given, though by our
more gallant standards it would seem to downgrade the Order of
Lenin.

One can see that the immediate aim is to try to ridicule the
British intelligence services while praising the Russian ones as the
last word in cunning and efficiency. Rival efforts to outwit and
deflate opponents will go on so long as states maintain intelligence
services . . .

Correct relations between states depend on the conventions
being observed. In plainer speech, they depend on certain pretences being kept up. One of the most useful conventions – or
pretences – is that you do not use the citizen of another country
as a spy. Or, if you do use him and he is found out, then you
disown him. No one is deceived. Not even the spy is surprised.
But relations between the two states can go on (not always, but
usually) because the little matter of attempted poison is ignored.

The Russians have chosen a bluffer, ruder manner with George
Blake. They have a man with an unspeakable record of treachery
that caused him his forty-two-year sentence in Britain; and they
gave him state honours. It is an odd way of cementing relations
with Britain, if that is what they want . . .

Blake's 'story' as recounted in *Izvestia* on 15 and 17 February
1970 consisted of two interviews by V. Lyadov and V. Rosin,
presumably journalists working for the paper. Each interview was
approximately two thousand words long both being mainly autobio-
graphical, the first ending with Blake's appointment as Vice-Consul
in Korea and the second with his arrest and imprisonment. In the
first he was introduced to the paper's readers as a heroic Soviet
intelligence officer, smartly dressed in a dark grey suit, neatly
outlining his athletic figure, and although he was over forty years
old as looking much younger. 'His dark hair with its reddish tints
is neatly combed and sets off his healthy colouring . . . He speaks
clearly and precisely. His Russian is near perfect.' He spoke at
length of his youth in Holland and his work for the Dutch Resistance
during the war and then of his work in Hamburg, later describing

how he was recruited into British secret intelligence (SIS). He dated the beginning of his sympathy with the Soviet Union to Winston Churchill's 'regrettably notorious Fulton speech' at Missouri in March 1946.

> It marked the beginning of the 'cold war' and the entire activity of SIS made a hundred and eighty degrees turn . . . I began to fear a revival of Nazi power and to think that all the sacrifices of the Soviet Union and the other socialist countries had been in vain.

When he was in Seoul as Vice-Consul in the British Legation, Blake said, he was instructed to collect intelligence on Siberia, Manchuria and Vladivostock.

> And this helped me to see with my own eyes the crime against humanity which was still being perpetuated, not by the Germans but by our allies, the Americans . . . The Korean people were waging a just war against an attack on their sovereignty. Thus, in just ten years I became an eye witness of, and partly a participant in, two wars. I am happy that I helped in my own way to unmask and suppress imperialist aggression and subversive actions; that even as a small cog in the wheel I managed to fight for peace, for the better future of mankind.

In the second interview Blake described his secret intelligence work after his return from Korea, first in London and then in Berlin, especially in the field of 'bugging'. In this context he mentioned the SIS–CIA meeting in London in December 1953 at which he was present when the Berlin tunnel operation code-named Gold was planned. Although the tunnel was not 'officially' discovered by the Soviet authorities until April 1956, nearly eighteen months later, Blake lost no time after the initial Anglo-American meeting to warn his Soviet contacts in London of Operation Gold. A meeting was arranged at a certain spot and Blake on approaching it saw some police waiting in a car. Should he go back? So he asked himself, or not turn up at the meeting, which would worry his 'comrades'? In the end he decided to take a chance and go on. In the event all was well, since it appeared that the police were merely on the track of an ordinary criminal.

Asked if he could give any other examples besides the secret tunnel of subversive activities directed against the Soviet Union in Berlin, Blake answered, 'Certainly.' He went on: 'This city was regarded by British and American intelligence as "the advanced post for espionage against the Russians". And it was then that SIS set up a special little shop not far from the border with the Soviet zone. SIS's purpose was to use the shop as a means of establishing contact with Soviet individuals, engaging them in commercial deals and finally recruiting them to work for the British. The shop owner was an agent of British intelligence, German by birth. As soon as a Russian appeared in the shop, the agent was to persuade him to place an order for goods which were in fact defective so as to ensure that the Russian would return.' Matters were so arranged that he would then meet a British representative who would take charge, cultivate his acquaintance and endeavour to recruit him to the British side.

'There was one amusing incident I can tell you regarding this shop,' Blake went on.

One day whilst on duty with SIS, I received the agreed signal from the shopowner: 'A Russian woman has come in!' I was to go at once and contact this customer. From the outside our acquaintance developed in a surprisingly easy manner. The woman called herself Nina and explained that she was a switchboard operator working at Soviet headquarters at Karlshorst. She appeared very interested in following up her acquaintance with me. However, further research revealed that 'Nina' was not Nina at all. She wasn't even Russian, but was working in West Berlin with an American colleague in the CIA . . . As for the shop, it was closed down shortly afterwards as 'an exceptionally unprofitable location'. You probably realize why? Besides I wouldn't want you to gain a wrong impression of the mutual relationship existing between the SIS and the CIA.

Blake gave other examples of how the Western countries spied on each other and also neutrals. In Paris, for instance, British intelligence obtained secret information on the French atomic energy programme, and in Sweden information on anti-aircraft defence, guided missiles and radioactive deposits. There were also SIS agents in West Germany's Foreign Affairs Ministry as well as in other federal government departments. Japanese diplomats and other Japanese living abroad were also to be cultivated to counteract the difficulties of establishing contact in Japan for language and other reasons, since Japanese living abroad were inclined to be lonely and this feeling should also be exploited.

'Having worked for many years in British intelligence,' one of the interviewers asked, 'you could no doubt throw light on how the SIS has used English citizens for subversive activities directed against the Soviet Union and other socialist states.'

'Yes,' Blake replied. '*Izvestia* has reported how SIS has used the BBC and many English newspaper reporters and journalists specializing in anti-Soviet propaganda and provocative falsehoods to further their aims . . . The affair of the English "businessman" Greville Wynne was known to be part of that plan.[1] British intelligence also attempted to recruit agents among tourists visiting socialist countries. What is more remarkable is that SIS enlisted people for this work without any kind of government agreement. Although using English diplomats or UN officials as intelligence agents did require permission from Britain's Ministry of Foreign Affairs, this was generally a pure formality.' Blake also described how defectors were used, formed, as he put it, from deserters and traitors from socialist countries.

One of the last questions put to him by the interviewers was: 'What did you think about when you were in prison?'

Blake thought for a moment or two before replying. 'There is always risk in the work of an intelligence agent,' he said. 'I knew

[1] Greville Wynne, who toured eastern Europe with a trade show, established contact in Moscow with Colonel Oleg Penkovsky, a GRU officer, who gave important information to MI6 and the CIA in London. Penkovsky and Wynne were tried and convicted of espionage in Moscow in 1963, Wynne getting eight years and Penkovsky death. After serving eleven months Wynne was exchanged for the Soviet agent Gordon Lonsdale, whereas Penkovsky was executed.

what I was in for and why. To the last I believed I had made the correct choice. Even in my London cell this thought gave me strength. From the start I gave myself two tasks; to keep fit in both mind and body so that I could eventually make my escape and continue the struggle. I got permission to complete my Arabic studies from the prison authorities and also practised yoga exercises . . . In prison I was certain my friends would not forget me. First of all, of course, there was my mother. She has always remained my closest and dearest friend. When I was arrested and given a forty-two-year sentence, she took my suits to the cleaners and then hung them in my wardrobe with mothballs. "Let them wait there for their master's return," she would tell her friends. "One day George will come back a free man!" What an optimistic and spirited woman!' (George did not come back to her, but it is likely that she took the suits with her when she visited her son in the Soviet Union for the first time in the summer of 1967.)

'George Blake is at present completing a book of memoirs,' the interview concluded, 'the memoirs of a Soviet agent working in the British Intelligence Service. We should add that Comrade Blake has been recognized for his selflessness in duty with the highest State awards – the Orders of Lenin and of the Red Banner for bravery.'

It is significant that nowhere in either of the interviews was there any mention made of Seán Bourke, although over a column was devoted to describing in detail Blake's escape from Wormwood Scrubs.

6

Izvestia's statement that George Blake was writing his memoirs naturally interested British and American publishers, notably Hodder & Stoughton in London and Doubleday in New York. Their inquiries led to an invitation to visit Moscow and read the script of Blake's work, for the world rights in which the Russians asked £30,000. Robin Denniston, then managing director of Hodder

& Stoughton, and a representative of Doubleday, accordingly arrived in Moscow in December 1971 and for the purpose of reading Blake's manuscript were accommodated in an office on the sixth floor of the Soviet Ministry of Foreign Trade, being supervised by several officials throughout the two hours it took them to read the work which was entitled *No Abiding City* and consisted of some 400 pages. Mr Denniston's report, which its author has kindly allowed the present writer to see, emphasized that there was not a great deal in the memoirs which was not already known or had been published elsewhere. Much of the first 150 pages were devoted by Blake to his life before he nominally joined the Foreign Office in 1948.

Some extracts from Mr Denniston's report are given below:

He emerges as serious, a bit priggish, brave, resourceful and full of potential. But he doesn't boast. His conduct in the Resistance in Holland has already been documented by Cookridge and maybe others. He does not add to this in any way. The tone in writing about internecine SIS feuding, the staple diet of ex-spies, is much more kind and less sophisticated than Philby. Meeting Menzies is presented as straight James Bond stuff. He seems to have no chip on his shoulder about the deb type girls around. He admires Peter Lunn for his work but has less time for his successor.

Then comes Korea, already fully documented by others. He has little to add. In fact he makes less of the bad conditions in Korea than Philip Deane. It was here that he was intellectually converted to Marxism . . . that coupled with his dislike of what he saw of the Syngman Rhee regime. No evidence that he was 'turned' at this point though. In fact barely a word of his so-called ideological friends from start to finish.

After Korea his FO career takes several steps forward and I would guess it was soon after his return that he became a Russian agent and, as he says at the end, photographed every document of any interest which came his way in the ten following years. That, and the very concealed claim that the discovery of the telecommunications tunnel under the Berlin wall was not a chance one (heavily censored at this point) are all we get of his real work. And this has already been asserted by Cookridge.

[178]

He goes on quite a lot about rivalries and post-war problems within the SIS. Those he names he praises – Dick White, Menzies, Lunn etc. Those he denigrates he doesn't mention by name assuming that they would not identify themselves and start proceedings. It's all interesting if you like that kind of thing. Should Y come under GCHQ or not? How the CIA were built up and then came to dominate the spy business. George Young's quoted views on spies.[1] A few presumably classified documents about our attitudes to how to penetrate the Russian intelligence and defence machine. The use of equipment or agents? (He prefers the personal touch and points out that most of the Peter Lunn bugging operations, like the second secretary at the Bulgarian embassy, were abortive because you couldn't hear what they said and even if you could they would probably not say anything interesting for months at a time.) . . .

These seem to me sensible middle-of-the-road views held by an intelligent and rising man, lacking the public school background, impatient with low standards of conduct, happily married, happily photographing everything after office hours. Still a bit of a prig. He says he has no abiding city, but his family are his sheet anchor; that and, later, the Communist view of society.

So we come to Berlin; he is much sketchier here than Cookridge as he mentions no names of any of his agents. One wonders if he has read the book. He criticizes Cookridge for his interpretations of his behaviour but displays no detailed knowledge of what has been written.[2] And incidentally he hasn't read Seán Bourke's book for his first chapter is a blow by blow account of his escape from Wormwood Scrubs, paralleling in most ways Bourke's book but of course with a lot of significant omissions. In Berlin he

---

[1] George Kennedy Young CB, had joined MI6 in 1946 and in Blake's time among other offices he held were Deputy Director to the MI6 chief 'Sinbad' Sinclair and Director of the Middle East Office. In 1984 he published a book on subversion.

[2] The book Robin Denniston has in mind was Cookridge's *George Blake Double Agent* published earlier in the year 1970 by Denniston's firm Hodder & Stoughton in paperback. Cookridge had written three other books about Blake of which Blake had only read one, *Shadow of a Spy* (published by Leslie Frewin in 1967) as mentioned in the text above: pp. 112, 116–7. This was not nearly as full and detailed as *George Blake Double Agent*.

describes the luxury shop set up to entice Russians, and the attempts he made to suborn Russians as agents for the West (these were all previously set up for him by his ideological friends). He names few names, but says that no agent of the West whom he betrayed was shot and the total prison years served by all he betrayed is less than the total Lord Chief Justice Parker handed out to him.

So to the language school in the Lebanon. When he had been rumbled and was asked to go back to London for routine talks, he debated whether to get out to Syria, tell his wife all and fly out to Russia. His instinct was to do this; but he didn't . . .

Blake tells us that he has remarried, has an excellent job which involves travelling through all the countries of the Soviet Union and leaves us with the suggestion, implicit in the title, that just as his life so far has been a series of distinctly framed events so his future may not continue exactly as at present. What he means I don't know. Possibly that Moscow life for the rest of his existence does not have an infinite appeal.

Robin Denniston was well qualified to report on Blake's work, by reason of his family's connection with secret intelligence, his father Commander A. G. ('Alastair') Denniston having been the legendary head of the Government code and cipher school at Bletchley Park during the war and his sister Margaret having been Kim Philby's secretary in MI6. Asked by the *Sunday Times* (16 January 1972) why he thought the Russians were making the Blake book available, Robin Denniston replied that he had an idea they were trying to drive a wedge between the Americans and the British. 'If it was published in America and not in Britain,' he was reported as saying, 'it could cause ill-feeling. I got the impression the Russians thought I'd gone to Moscow to put a damper on the Americans. At the end of our meeting they gave the American a big gold fountain pen, and me a small Parker biro.'

When Vice-Admiral Sir Norman Denning, the Secretary of the Defence and Broadcasting Committee responsible for D notices, was informed of the large sum which the Russians were asking for the world rights, he commented: 'The publisher who gives that kind of money to the Russians wouldn't be very popular. They could put it straight back into espionage.'

In the event Robin Denniston and the American publishers – Doubleday had been joined by Dutton – together offered £4,000 for the world rights, which was really more than the book was worth, in view of the fact that its contents were little more than an expansion of the two *Izvestia* interviews already quoted. Doubleday was inclined to offer more if 'Blake peppered it up a bit'. But from the Soviet point of view this was not practicable. So the matter was dropped and it has never been revived. Nor is it likely to be. For one thing it was neither as informative nor as interesting as Kim Philby's memoir of his early life and his years in MI6 *My Secret War*, which appeared in Britain in 1968 and was later published in Russian in the Soviet Union.

Since they were both British expatriates as well as holders of the Orders of Lenin and the Red Banner, it was inevitable that Blake and Philby should meet. Philby had an attractive dacha in the woods outside Moscow and the couple would often meet there for Sunday lunch with their respective wives and other guests. Philby, having taken up with his fellow-spy Donald Maclean's American wife Melinda, discarded her after a two-year liaison and she went back to her husband for a time before eventually returning to America. Philby's fourth wife was a Russian called Nina, and Blake's second, also a Russian, whom he married a year or so after Seán Bourke's departure from Moscow, was known as Ida; he had a son, Mischa, by her.

Henri Curiel, Blake's Egyptian Communist uncle, with whom he may well have kept in touch, since Curiel is thought to have worked for the KGB after his expulsion from Egypt by President Nasser, eventually went to live in France where he was involved with several revolutionary organizations and is believed to have supplied the Russians with information about them. In May 1978 he was murdered, aged sixty-three, in Paris by unidentified gunmen, undoubtedly extreme right-wing terrorists.

Maclean died in Moscow in March 1983, aged sixty-nine. He was given an impressive funeral by his comrades in the KGB and the government research institute where he worked. But no member of his family was present, nor were Philby and Blake, although no doubt they read *Izvestia*'s tribute to him for having 'performed great services in the struggle against fascism'. The other British traitor Guy Burgess had died twenty years previously, so that this now leaves only George Blake and Kim Philby as the remaining super-spies. Blake now being sixty-five and Philby ten years older, Blake approaching retiring age and Philby having already retired.

George Blake continues to live in comfort in a spacious Moscow flat with his wife and son and he is well paid by Soviet standards with a generous pension to look forward to. But one cannot help wondering, as he looks back on his past life of treachery which he must sometimes do, whether he is a happy man. Can any traitor be so?

POSTSCRIPT

In November 1987, following press allegations, the Conservative MP Andrew MacKay asked the Commons leader in the House John Wakeham if he thought there should be a debate on the claims that the actress Vanessa Redgrave and other CND members helped to finance the operation to spring Blake from prison. Mr Wakeham side-stepped the question by telling Mr Mackay that he could no doubt find out a way to debate the matter. About the same time Seán Bourke's solicitor in Ireland John Gore-Grimes confirmed the allegation about Miss Redgrave, but stated that Bourke had told him that Miss Redgrave did not know what the money she contributed was being used for. 'I believe what Bourke told me,' the solicitor added. 'He couldn't have made it up.'

The British double agent Harold (Kim) Philby died in Moscow on 11 May, 1988, at the age of 76. He was buried with full military honours at Kuntsevo cemetery in the western suburbs of the Soviet capital. While referred to simply as Comrade Kim in the funeral orations, it is understood that he ended his career as a general in the KGB, although no reference was made to his rank during the funeral. No doubt Blake was among the mourners on this occasion.

Select Bibliography

A Unpublished sources

Kenneth Hugh de Courcy (Duc de Grantmesnil). Papers in the Hoover Institution Archives, Stanford University, California.

    (1) George Blake Memorandum written by de Courcy in Wormwood Scrubs Prison c 1967.

    (2) Interview with de Courcy by Charles G. Palm, Acting Archivist of the Hoover Institution, 6 April 1983.

Robin D. Denniston, Report on Blake's autobiography *No Abiding City* for Hodder & Stoughton, 22 December 1971. In the possession of the Revd Robin Denniston, Oxford University Press.

Kevin O'Connor, 'A Death in January'. Radio documentary on life of Seán Bourke broadcast on RTE, Dublin. Cassette in the possession of Kevin O'Connor, Dublin. It contains among others two brief conversations between Bourke and Blake by walkie-talkie in October 1966, relating to the tools required by Blake to facilitate his escape from prison, such as a car jack. Bourke did not quote these in his book *The Springing of George Blake*, since he retained them as evidence of his actions in the event of his talks being doubted afterwards.

B Published sources

Christopher Andrew, *Secret Service* (London: Heinemann, 1985).

Atticus, On Blake's autobiography, *Sunday Times*, 16 January 1972: London.

Seán Bourke, *The Springing of George Blake* (London: Cassell, 1970).

Andrew Boyle, *The Climate of Treason* (London: Hutchinson, 1979).

E. H. Cookridge, *Traitor Betrayed* (London: Pan Books, 1962).

— *Shadow of a Spy* (London: Leslie Frewin, 1967).

— *The Many Sides of George Blake, Esq* (New York: Vertrex, 1970).

— *George Blake Double Agent* (London: Hodder & Stoughton, 1970).

Henri Curiel, 'Assassination', *L'Express*, 8/14 May 1978: Paris.

Richard Deacon, *A History of the Russian Secret Service* (London: Muller, 1972).
— *The British Connection* (London: Hamish Hamilton, 1979).
Philip Deane, *Captive in Korea* (London: Hamish Hamilton, 1953).
Christopher Dobson, and Ronald Payne, *The Dictionary of Espionage* (London: Harrap, 1984).
Izvestia, 'Operation "Gold" and Others' (Moscow: 15/17 February 1970; in Russian).
Philip Knightley, *The Second Oldest Profession* (London: Andre Deutsch, 1986).
Norman Lucas, *The Great Spy Ring* (London: Arthur Baker, 1966).
Donald McCormick, *The Master Book of Spies* (London: Hodder Causton, 1973).
Kim Philby, *My Silent War* (London: Macgibbon & Kee, 1968).
Chapman Pincher, *Inside Story* (London: Sidgwick & Jackson, 1978).
— *Their Trade is Treachery* (London: Sidgwick & Jackson, 1981).
— *Too Secret Too Long* (London: Sidgwick & Jackson, 1984).
Ronald Seth, *Encyclopedia of Espionage* (London: New English Library, 1972).
John Vassall, *Vassall: The Autobiography of a Spy* (London: Sidgwick & Jackson, 1975).
Nigel West, *A Matter of Trust: MI5 1945–72* (London: Weidenfeld & Nicolson, 1982).
Dame Rebecca West, *The Meaning of Treason* (Harmondsworth: Penguin Books, 1965).

Index

The following abbreviations are used:
GB for George Blake; SB for Seán Bourke.

MI6 – *cont.*
  recruits GB, 28, 29, 30, 43–4
  and SIS, 48, 51, 52, 62, 174–6,
    178–9
  recalls GB to London, 50, 53
  interrogates GB, 54–5
Molody, Konon Trofimovitch, *see*
  Lonsdale, Gordon
Montgomery, General, 27–8
Morrison, Herbert (Lord), 17
Mountbatten, Earl, 90

Nasser, President, 44, 51, 181
News of the World, The, 155
Newton, Andrew, 74–5
No Abiding City, 178
nuclear energy, 13, 18, 145, 176

Official Secrets Act, 12, 54, 158
O'Keefe, Mr Justice, 169–71
Owen, Norman, 31, 38, 42

Parker, Lord Chief Justice, 11, 14,
  17, 18, 58, 180
Paul, Mr Justice, 17
Peake, Iris, 30–1
Peake, Osbert, MP, 30–1
Penkovsky, Oleg, 59, 176
Perruche, Georges, 33, 40
Philby, Kim, 43, 62, 103, 109, 146,
  153, 172, 178, 180, 181, 182
Philby, St John (1885–1960), 62
Pincher, Chapman, 19, 184
Popov, Peter, 48, 49
Porter, Pat, 63, 89, 93, 95, 96, 97,
  104, 105, 110
Portland Spy Ring, 19, 52, 58, 59

Quinlan, Monsignor Thomas, 36, 41,
  42

Red Banner, Order of, 103, 146, 173,
  177, 181
Reynolds, Anne, 71, 89, 90, 92, 93,
  94, 95, 96
Reynolds, Michael, 63, 70–1, 78, 85,
  87, 88–9, 90, 92–7, 99, 105, 110
Rhee, Dr Syngman, 32–3, 178

Ridgway, General Mathew, 39
Rosin, V., 173
Rotterdam, 20–3
Russell, Bertrand, 63, 98
Russia, *see* Soviet Union

Schmidt, Ursula, 47
Scott, Norman, 74
Semichastny, V. Y., 103, 104, 108
Serov, Ivan, 47
Seyss-Inquart, Arthur von, 24
Shadow of a Spy (Cookridge), 112,
  116–17, 179, 183
Shelepin, Alexander, 103
Shergold, Harold, 54
Shinwell, Emmanuel, 17
Sinclair, Sir John, 43–4, 52, 179
SIS, *see* MI6
Soviet Union, 13, 19, 28–30, 48–9,
  51–2, 75, 93, 94, 101–54,
  155–67, 172–7, 180–2
Special Operations Executive (SOE),
  24, 25, 26, 27
special watch prisoners, 56–7, 59, 60
Springing of George Blake, The (Seán
  Bourke), 9, 151, 171, 183
Stalin, Joseph, 62, 108, 115, 140–1
Stalin, Svetlana, 108
'Stan' (KGB officer), 101–54, 155–67
Stockton, Lord, *see* Macmillan,
  Harold
Suez crisis, 51
Sunday Express, 112
Sweden, 176
Syria, 53

'Tairova', 49
Tcheka, 146
Templer, Major-General Gerald, 29
Thomson, Rear-Admiral George
  Pirie, 11, 19
Thorpe, Jeremy, 74
Times, The, 172–3
Truman, President, 35, 39

United Nations, 35, 40, 46

'Valentin' (KGB officer), 152, 153

A TANGLED WEB
H. Montgomery Hyde

No event seizes the public imagination, fills the pages of
the press and the conversations of the gossips like a Sex
Scandal; the greatest and most powerful brought low by the
most interesting of subjects.

And here there is much to satisfy even the most salacious of
curiosities, an informed, informative and entertaining
chronicle of lecherous lords, perverted politicians, seducing
celebrities and discreditable diplomats. From Lord
Melbourne's enthusiasm for flagellation to the public
revelations about Cecil Parkinson and his private secretary,
via Parnell, Profumo and Lambton, Wilde, Driberg and Thorpe,
the author unravels the tangled web of sexual intrigue with
lucidity and wit.

'This disgustingly entertaining book'
BOOKS & BOOKMEN

'This book has all the scandalous details'
TODAY

Futura Publications
Non-Fiction
ISBN 0 7088 3256 3

THE TRUTH TWISTERS
Richard Deacon

The origins of disinformation stretch back centuries before
Christ. But it has become uniquely part of the late twentieth
century, practised on a hitherto undreamed-of scale by the
Soviet bloc and to a lesser extent by the West.

*The mysterious Wehrwoelfe — a Nazi army which refused to
 surrender or a fabrication?

*What is the truth about the dangers of nuclear power?

*Why are certain American UFO documents still classified?

*The plot of Frederick Forsyth's *The Fourth Protocol* — could
 it be a way of warning the Russians not to attempt any
 such operation in this country?

*Why is the Church silent on the fate of Lebanese Christians?

*Was the Sino-Soviet split pure fiction?

This absorbing, thought-provoking survey contains much new
and first-hand material. Disinformation threatens not only the
well-being of individuals but the security of nations, and we
must all become alerted to its dangers.

'a fascinating and quite alarming study of the politics of
untruth'
LONDON STANDARD

'the comprehensive story of disinformation'
DAILY EXPRESS

Futura Publications
Non-Fiction
ISBN 0 7088 3644 5

Futura now offers an exciting range of quality fiction
and non-fiction by both established and new authors.
All of the books in this series are available from good
bookshops, or can be ordered from the following
address:

Futura Books
Cash Sales Department
P.O. Box 11
Falmouth
Cornwall, TR10 9EN.

Please send cheque or postal order (no currency), and
allow 60p for postage and packing for the first book plus
25p for the second book and 15p for each additional book
ordered up to a maximum charge of £1.50 in U.K.

B.F.P.O. customers please allow 60p for the first book,
25p for the second book plus 15p per copy for the next
7 books, thereafter 9p per book.

Overseas customers, including Eire, please allow £1.25
for postage and packing for the first book, 75p for the second
book and 28p for each subsequent title ordered.